sweet nursery chic

susan cousineau

KRAUSE PUBLICATIONS
CINCINNATI, OHIO

mycraftivity.com
connect. create. explore.

Published by Krause Publications, an imprint of F+W Media, Inc., 4700 East Galbraith Road, Cincinnati, Ohio, 45236. (800) 289-0963. First Edition.

Other fine Krause Publications titles are available from your local bookstore, craft supply store, online retailer or visit our Web site at www.fwmedia.com.

13   12   11   10   09   5   4   3   2   1

DISTRIBUTED IN CANADA BY FRASER DIRECT
100 Armstrong Avenue
Georgetown, ON, Canada L7G 5S4
Tel: (905) 877-4411

DISTRIBUTED IN THE U.K. AND EUROPE BY DAVID & CHARLES
Brunel House, Newton Abbot, Devon, TQ12 4PU, England
Tel: (+44) 1626 323200, Fax: (+44) 1626 323319
E-mail: postmaster@davidandcharles.co.uk

DISTRIBUTED IN AUSTRALIA BY CAPRICORN LINK
P.O. Box 704, S. Windsor NSW, 2756 Australia
Tel: (02) 4577-3555

Library of Congress Cataloging in Publication Data
Cousineau, Susan.
  Sweet nursury chic / Susan Cousineau.—1st ed.
    p. cm.
  Includes index.
  ISBN-13: 978-1-4402-0401-2 (pbk. : alk. paper)
  ISBN-10: 1-4402-0401-2 (pbk. : alk. paper)
  1. Sewing. 2. Nurseries—Equipment and supplies. 3. Infants' supplies. I. Title.
  TT715.C678 2009
  646.4'06—dc22
                       2009018372

Edited by Christine Doyle and Rachel Scheller
Designed by Michelle Thompson
Production coordinated by Matt Wagner
Photography by Al Parrish

about the author

Author and designer Susan Cousineau began her professional design career in 1993. Susan's fresh and whimsical style was an instant hit at her first industry trade show, and her work soon graced the covers of numerous craft and home décor magazines. Susan has authored twenty books and is in the process of developing her own enchanting line of sewing patterns. For further information, visit Susan's storybook studio at www.sweetchicdesign.com.

metric conversion chart

To convert	to	multiply by
Inches	Centimeters	2.54
Centimeters	Inches	0.39
Feet	Centimeters	30.48
Centimeters	Feet	0.0328
Yards	Meters	0.9
Meters	Yards	1.1

contents

introduction

Now more than ever parents are searching for innovative and savvy do-it-yourself ideas for creating their dream nurseries and kids' spaces. And it's no wonder! In addition to saving oodles of cash, sewing for tiny tots gives you the opportunity to personalize your child's surroundings with colors, fabrics and embellishments that complement your own unique style. You can create a magical destination, a creative environment that inspires your child's imagination in exciting new ways, without ever leaving home.

Sweet Nursery Chic offers a multitude of fresh and fun ideas to create that perfectly coordinated space, from quilts and wall hangings to pillows, blankets and accessories. Regardless of your personal decorating style, whether it's classic, whimsical, modern or trendy, you're sure to find a theme to tickle your fancy. I've included plenty of tips for creating unforgettable baby shower gifts as well as fun project variations to inspire you to create all sorts of sweet treats and decorating delights with those leftover fabric scraps.

The first two sections of this book provide everything you need to know about the materials, tools and techniques needed to complete the projects, including choosing the perfect fabric and fast appliqué techniques. I've included a handy Stitch Guide (see page 17) for those who are new to embroidery stitching techniques. Of course, those who are short on time can always use a sewing machine instead! And because child safety should always be a priority, I've also added important safety tips for sewing trims and embellishments and decorating the nursery.

Once you're familiar with the basic supplies and techniques, it's time for the creative fun to begin! The chapters to follow feature ten fabulous décor and gift collections, from charming princess frogs and blushing bunnies to funky monkeys and goofy gators! When selecting your favorite theme, be sure to make it your own by choosing colors and prints that reflect your personal style. And remember the most important thing of all—have fun and share your sweet stitches with lots of love!

Happy stitching!

Materials and Tools

In this section, you'll find a list of the general supplies needed to complete these charming nursery projects. Since most of the projects require these same basic necessities, they will be listed here instead of repeated in the individual collections.

tools and equipment

Sewing machine: A sewing machine is a must for assembling most of the projects. You can use your machine as desired to sew ribbon and rickrack trims and to sew around appliqués, if this is preferred to hand-stitching and embroidery.

Iron and ironing board: An iron is necessary for pressing fabric and seams and for fusible web appliqué.

Rotary cutter, cutting mat and transparent, grid-lined ruler: These tools are used for cutting precise shapes, such as squares, strips and rectangles, quickly and accurately.

Disappearing-ink pens (air- or water-soluble): These are great for tracing pattern shapes directly onto fabric, transferring pattern details for stitching and making tiny reference marks for the placement of appliqué pieces. Most often, these marks can be removed with a damp cloth. It's best to remove any marks prior to pressing your fabric.

Pencil and permanent marker: Use a pencil to trace patterns onto the paper side of fusible web. A permanent marker is best for tracing pattern shapes onto template plastic.

Sharp scissors: Always use a pair of sharp, high-quality scissors when cutting fabric. To maintain their sharpness, use a separate pair of scissors for cutting paper and heavier materials such as template plastic or poster board.

Seam ripper: This is an indispensable tool for removing stitches quickly and neatly.

Measuring tape: Use a flexible measuring tape to measure fabric, trim lengths and accurately place appliqué pieces.

Hand-sewing and embroidery needles: Use hand-sewing needles to sew trims and seams and embroidery needles to apply decorative embroidered accents. Choose the size of the needle based on the fabric and/or trims you are stitching and the number of strands of thread or floss you are using.

Straight pins (1½" [4cm], large-headed): Use straight pins for the piecing and assembling of quilts, wall hangings, pillows, bibs, etc. A magnetic pin holder is a handy tool for storing your pins and preventing them from scattering onto your work space.

Fray preventative: A liquid version such as Fray Check is best for applying onto the ends of ribbons and rickrack trim. A spray such as Fray Stop is best for covering larger areas such as the edges of a chenille wall hanging.

Quilt basting spray or fabric spray adhesive: Use these sprays to baste your felt and chenille appliqué pieces for stitching and to assemble the layers of quilts, wall hangings and bibs. Keep in mind that for smaller appliqué pieces there are numerous nonspray basting products available, such as fabric and appliqué glues (in liquid versions or glue sticks). Feel free to use your preferred technique.

Regular or lightweight paper-backed fusible web: Fusible webs such as HeatnBond Lite and Wonder Under are used to bond appliqué shapes onto background fabric quickly and easily.

Permanent fabric adhesive (such as Fabri-Tac): This product is a great alternative to stitching your fabric trims. There are other brands available; use the one that works best for you.

Template plastic or poster board: Use these if making permanent templates for your appliqué patterns.

fabric

A wide variety of fabrics were used to create the projects in this book, including:

Cotton: Cotton fabric is a favorite among sewers, quilters and appliqué artists. It is super easy to sew and is the perfect choice when using fusible web appliqué. The colors and prints you choose will be the most important factors in determining the overall look and feel of your collection. Refer to the Style Guide on page 11 for further information on choosing cotton print fabrics.

Wool felt: The wool felt appliqués add a fun texture to the projects. Wool felt does not fray, so it is easy to cut pattern pieces directly from the fabric. If you will be laundering your project, it's important to prewash the wool felt as it shrinks substantially when washed. If you are unable to find a particular color of felt, you can always substitute it with fleece or cotton.

Chenille: Chenille fabrics add texture, softness and contrast to your designs. They also add timeless vintage style, which contrasts nicely when combined with some of the bolder and more modern prints, such as in the Mango Tango collection (see page 76).

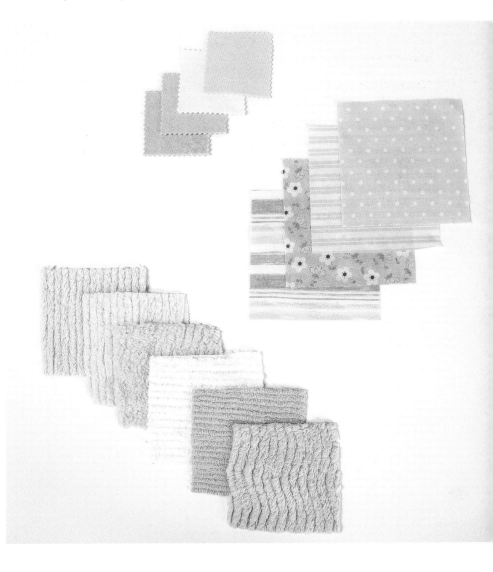

miscellaneous materials

Cotton embroidery floss: Embroidery floss is used for hand-stitching details and embroidering around appliqué shapes. It is available in skeins with six strands wound together. DMC and Anchor are the two most popular brands. (Although I list DMC colors, there are several online color conversion charts that can assist you in selecting a similar color using the Anchor brand.)

Embroidery hoop: A hoop is used for hand embroidery and is purely optional.

Quilt batting: Batting adds thickness and dimension to quilts, bibs, wall hangings, etc. Both cotton and polyester varieties work well, and each has its own advantages. Cotton is natural and easy to work with, while polyester is more lightweight and inexpensive.

Polyester fiberfill and pillow inserts: These are used for stuffing pillows and other decorative accents.

Embellishment materials: Ribbons, rickrack, buttons, pom-poms, marabou boa, ribbon rosebuds and flower trims all add charm and a unique touch to your collection.

Techniques

This introductory section provides a detailed overview of the basic techniques used to complete these fun nursery and kids' décor collections. You'll learn everything from how to choose and prepare your fabric to quick and easy appliqué and stitching techniques. You'll also find detailed instructions for completing your quilts, pillows and wall hangings, making it easy to refer to this section for each of the design collections. I've also included lots of helpful tips to make your "sew" easy projects even easier!

Choosing Cotton Prints

STYLE GUIDE

Some style choices for babies and kids include:

- Classic/Traditional: Soft pastel colors and neutral shades; prints such as ginghams, plaids, calicos and small florals

- Whimsical: Bright colors and playful prints such as stripes, polka dots and geometrics

- Modern/Contemporary: Bright and bold geometrics, large florals and trendy colors and prints

- Themed: Novelty prints or colors that reflect a theme

Don't feel the need to limit your fabric choices to one particular style. Most of the collections in this book use a combination of decorating styles, which adds visual interest and contrast to the design. For example, the Bayou Buddies collection (see page 96) combines classic prints such as ginghams and plaids with whimsical polka dots and modern geometrics.

COLOR VALUE AND SCALE

Two additional considerations when choosing your fabrics are the color value and the scale of the prints. Contrast is important in any design and is best achieved with an assortment of the two. Use a variety of light, medium and dark color values so your design does not look washed out. Also avoid using too many large prints as your design may look busy and be hard on the eyes.

choosing your fabric

A wide variety of fabrics were used to complete the projects in this book, namely cotton prints, wool felt and chenille. Combining these different varieties creates interesting texture and contrast. You can use my fabric selections as a guide, but feel free to change colors and prints to reflect your personal taste and to complement your room décor. Refer to the Style Guide on page 11 for tips on choosing cotton prints.

If a particular type of fabric, such as chenille or wool felt, is unavailable, you can easily adapt the project using some creative substitutions. For the wool felt appliqués, you can substitute hard-to-find colors with a plain cotton or fleece fabric.

Chenille backgrounds can also be replaced with a cotton print or wool felt fabric (see the variation of the Jungle Chic Monkey Pillow on page 64). If you are replacing a chenille appliqué with a cotton print, simply use the fusible web appliqué technique instead of basting. One exception for substituting chenille is a wall hanging that is sewn entirely of chenille fabric. If you are unable to find a particular color of chenille at your local quilt or fabric shop, check out the online resource section on page 126. You can always consider dyeing white chenille fabric since it is widely available in most fabric stores.

When purchasing your fabric, keep in mind that yardage is based on standard 44–45" (112–114cm) widths for cotton and cotton/polyester blend prints.

As for color and print choices, don't feel limited by those used in the sample projects. You can easily vary your color palette and even the types of fabrics used if certain ones are not available in your local area.

The projects in this book are a great way to use up fabric scraps and fat quarters. I listed exact measurement sizes rather than yardage in the project materials lists. If purchasing your fabric by the yard, simply divide the number of inches by 36 to find the yardage. Keep in mind that it's always best to overestimate the fabric requirements to allow for selvage, uneven cuts and shrinkage.

preparing your fabric

Whether or not to prewash your fabric is a personal choice and depends on many factors. Here are some questions to consider:

Is the project for decorative use only or will it be laundered? If laundered, it's best to prewash fabrics to prevent shrinkage and to test for possible bleeding. I gener-ally do not prewash fabrics for projects that are for decorative use only.

Will the project be in direct contact with the baby or small child? Prewashing fabrics will remove any harsh chemicals that may possibly irritate their skin.

What are the manufacturer's instructions for the products you are using? For example, some manufacturers of fusible web products recommend that fabrics be prewashed for best results. However, I have achieved satisfactory results using these products without prewashing them. To be sure, you can first test a small piece of fabric to determine whether prewashing is necessary.

cutting your fabric

Here are some tips for cutting your fabric pieces:

Be sure to iron your fabric to remove all folds and creases prior to cutting.

When cutting precise shapes, such as squares, strips and rectangles, use a rotary cutter, mat and transparent grid-lined ruler.

Use sharp, high-quality fabric scissors for cutting appliqué shapes from the felt or fused fabric. Do not use the same scissors for cutting cardboard, template plastic and paper.

For the quilts, I find it preferable to cut and assemble the individual blocks first, then cut borders, bindings, backing, etc. However, feel free to modify the order of the instructions to best suit your preferred cutting methods and techniques.

appliqué

The design motifs featured in each collection are created using quick and easy appliqué techniques. The term *appliqué* simply means to cut one fabric shape and adhere it onto another. When layering the appliqué pieces onto the background fabric, you can use the finished project photo and the dotted lines on the patterns as an indication of the order of placement. (Dotted lines indicate that the appliqué piece lies underneath.) It is often helpful with some of the more detailed appliqués to use a disappearing-ink pen to mark the placement of the pieces with tiny reference lines.

There are two basic appliqué techniques you will use depending on the type of fabric used in the pattern motif. Most of the designs feature a combination of the two techniques.

Fusible Web Appliqué

The fusible web technique is a simple way to add decorative appliqués to your sewing projects. Just follow these steps.

1 Trace the pattern shape onto the paper side of the fusible web.

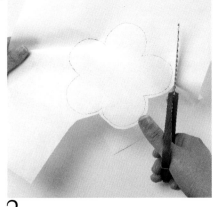

2 Cut out the pieces, leaving approximately ¼" (6mm) around the shapes.

3 Following the manufacturer's instructions, iron the fusible web pieces, paper side-up, onto the wrong side of the chosen fabrics. Let them cool.

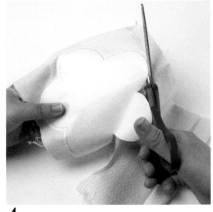

4 Cut out the pieces along the traced lines.

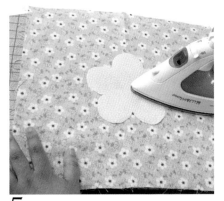

5 Remove the paper backing, then fuse the appliqué pieces following the manufacturer's instructions.

Here are some additional points to remember when using the fusible web appliqué technique:

≈✲ Be sure to purchase a regular or lightweight fusible web to allow for decorative stitching around the edges. The heavier weight or ultra-hold fusible webs are for no-sew appliqué projects.

≈✲ Always remember to follow the manufacturer's instructions as they may vary slightly between brands.

≈✲ Remember that asymmetrical shapes will appear in the opposite direction when fused onto the background fabric because they are being traced from the back (paper side) of the fusible web. You needn't worry about this for the majority of the patterns because most of the shapes are symmetrical and, therefore, similar on both sides (e.g., circles, ear shapes, wings, ground pieces, etc.). There will be a special note in the pattern insert to remind you when a shape must be reversed for one of the block designs.

Basting Appliqué

For wool felt, fleece and chenille fabrics, I find it easiest to apply the appliqué pieces using a simple basting technique. Although there are numerous basting materials and techniques to choose from, my preferred method is to simply apply a temporary fabric spray adhesive or quilter's basting spray onto the back of the fabric shape, then press it into place. In addition to spray basting, there are numerous fabric glues on the market that work well with appliqué. I find that spray basting is the quickest alternative, but feel free to use any technique that works best for you. Note that most spray adhesives provide only a temporary bond to secure the fabric shape for stitching. This allows you to reposition the piece until you are satisfied with the placement. As always, be sure to follow the manufacturer's instructions for your specific brand of fabric adhesive.

Here are some additional points to remember when basting your appliqué pieces:

≈✲ The dotted lines on the patterns indicate the order of placement for the fabric pieces (dotted lines appear underneath). You can use these dotted lines and the finished project photo as guides when basting the layered fabric motifs.

≈✲ When instructed to baste a particular motif (e.g., giraffe) assume that you will be basting all of the giraffe pieces (e.g., nose, spots, horns) as they appear in the pattern.

making appliqué templates

Sometimes you'll find that having a pemanent template of a pattern comes in handy. Here are some helpful tips. (Keep in mind that these tips are optional when using the fusible web appliqué technique. As you can see from Step 1 on page 13, the shape can be traced onto the fusible web directly without the use of a permanent template.)

I find it easiest to transfer patterns onto fabric using a permanent template cut from poster board, cardstock or template plastic. When you use a template, you can trace the pattern shape onto the fabric quickly and precisely, which ensures accurate piecing. It also saves valuable time when you are using the same pattern for multiple pieces in the collection.

Because template plastic is transparent, you can trace over the pattern in one easy step using a permanent marker. Then use sharp scissors (but not your fabric scissors) to cut the shape along the traced lines. If you don't have template plastic available, you can trace the shape onto poster board or cardstock. Simply cut out the photocopied patterns from the book and trace around them or use tracing and transfer paper.

Tracing Your Appliqué Templates

After you've made your template, use a pencil to trace the shape onto the paper side of the fusible web, or use a disappearing-ink pen to trace around the template directly onto your felt, fleece or chenille fabric. Then cut the shape from the fabric along the traced lines using a pair of sharp scissors.

Remember to reverse the tracing of your template for asymmetrical shapes as indicated in the pattern insert.

appliqué stitching techniques

You can finish the edges of your appliqué pieces using either hand embroidery or machine stitching, or perhaps a combination of the two. I chose to hand embroider the designs to give them a handcrafted look. Refer to the Stitch Guide diagram on page 17 for a visual illustration of the embroidery stitches used to complete the projects in this book. Stitches used include the blanket stitch, running stitch, backstitch, straight stitch, satin stitch, cross stitch and French knot.

Use a disappearing-ink pen to trace facial features and other hand-stitched details.

To save time, you can use your preferred machine stitch (e.g., zigzag, blanket or satin) around the edges of the appliqués and use hand stitching for the facial elements and other decorative details.

≋✻ Tip: Most of the projects in this book are for decorative use only. However, you may want to use a more secure machine stitch for appliqués on bibs, blankets and other items that may be laundered repeatedly.

As noted in the project instructions, use two strands of floss for all embroidery stitching unless otherwise indicated. Generally four strands of floss are used when stitching directly onto chenille.

safety first!

Most of the projects in this book were designed for decorative use only and are not meant to be in direct contact with babies and small children (the exceptions being bibs and blankets). The quilts, pillows and blankets placed in cribs throughout the book are for photographic purposes only. Never put your baby to bed with these soft bedding items as they may present a serious safety hazard.

Remember that embellishments such as buttons and other trims may pose a choking hazard to tots, especially those under the age of three, so be sure to take the appropriate safety precautions. You may wish to forgo the trims altogether, using stitching instead to add the design elements (e.g., a satin stitch for a nose instead of a button). If adding decorative trims, use heavy thread or even dental floss to secure them. Test trims by pulling on them as hard as you can to make sure they are securely fastened. And as always, make sure children are adequately supervised when in contact with any embellished project.

general instructions: quilts

Refer to these basic instructions to piece, assemble and bind your quilts.

1 Piece the quilt top

When piecing the blocks of your quilt, place the fabric pieces right sides together and sew using a ¼" (6mm) seam allowance.

Refer to the finished project photo to piece the three rows of each quilt. Then sew the three rows together to form the quilt top.

Press the seam allowances in one direction, preferably toward the darker fabric or in the direction that will create the least amount of bulk. Pressing seam allowances in opposite directions makes it easier to line up the seams in each row.

2 Add the border

Cut four 3" (8cm) strips along the width of the fabric.

Sew the side borders first. Press and trim.

Sew the borders to the top and bottom. Press and trim.

3 Assemble the layers

Cut the backing fabric and batting several inches larger than the finished size of your quilt top.

Baste the batting in between the top and bottom layers of the quilt with the wrong sides of the quilt top and backing facing together. Smooth out any wrinkles on the fabric and batting.

Pin the three layers together, then stitch-in-the-ditch along the seams (or quilt as desired).

Trim the batting and backing fabric even with the edges of the quilt top.

4 Add a hanging sleeve

Sewing a sleeve onto the back of your quilt makes it easy to display using a rod or dowel. It's also a safe method for hanging your quilt as it prevents potential distortion and damage, which other hanging methods sometimes cause. It may also keep your quilt hanging straighter and flatter against the wall.

To determine the size of fabric required for your hanging sleeve, first measure the width of your quilt. You will want to cut a strip of fabric approximately 1"–2" (3cm–5cm) less than this width measurement.

Since you will be folding the sleeve prior to sewing, you'll want to double the finished size. I decided to use a 3" (8cm) sleeve, so to double that measurement, I cut a 6" (15cm) wide strip.

Fold the fabric strip right sides together, aligning the long edges. Sew along the short edges using a ¼" (6mm) seam allowance. Trim the corners, turn right side out and press. Center the sleeve onto the back so that the top raw edges of the quilt and sleeve are even. Stitch the sleeve to the quilt with an approximate ⅛"–¼" (3mm-6mm) seam allowance.

After the binding is sewn (see Step 5), hand-stitch the bottom edge of the sleeve onto the quilt.

5 Add the binding

Cut five 2½" (6cm) wide binding strips along the width of the fabric.

Sew the strips right sides together with diagonal seams (i.e., at a 45° angle) into one continuous strip. Trim the excess fabric, leaving a ¼" (6mm) seam allowance. Press the seams open.

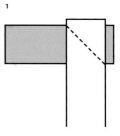

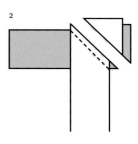

Press the binding strip in half lengthwise, wrong sides together.

Beginning in the middle of one side and with raw edges aligned, pin the binding to the quilt top.

Leaving a tail approximately 8" (20cm) long at the beginning, sew the binding to the quilt top using a ¼" (6mm) seam allowance.

Stop stitching ¼" (6mm) from the corner of the quilt and backstitch. Remove the quilt. Fold up the binding strip at a 45° angle, away from the quilt, then fold it down even with the raw edge of the quilt. Begin stitching at the fold, stitching through all layers. Continue sewing around the quilt, repeating the same process for each corner.

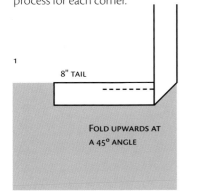

1

8" TAIL

FOLD UPWARDS AT
A 45° ANGLE

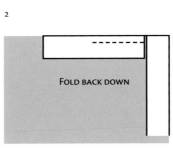

2

FOLD BACK DOWN

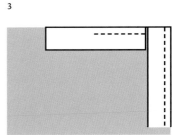

3

Bring the folded edge of the binding strip to the back of the quilt and hand-stitch the binding in place.

stitch guide

Follow the stitch illustrations to bring the needle up at odd numbers and down at even numbers.

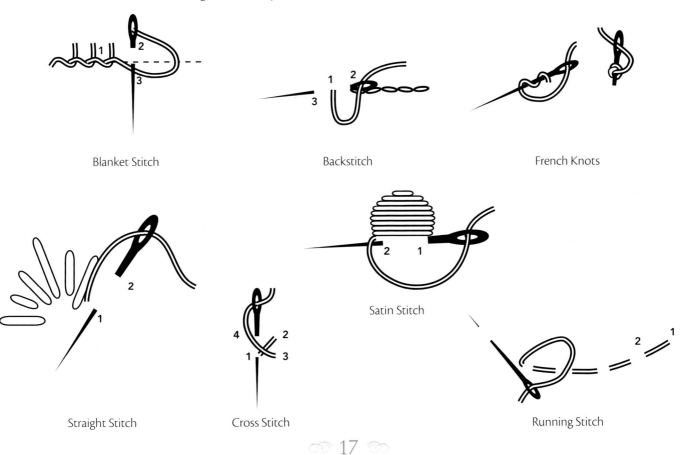

Blanket Stitch

Backstitch

French Knots

Satin Stitch

Straight Stitch

Cross Stitch

Running Stitch

general instructions: pillows

Note: I use a ¼" (6mm) seam allowance for the 14" × 14" (36cm × 36cm) square pillows. However, if you prefer to use a larger ½" (13mm) seam allowance, just adjust your fabric measurements accordingly. (Cut 14½" [37cm] squares for the pillow front and back instead of 14" [36cm], and 5½" [14cm] squares for the patchwork pillow fronts instead of 5" [13cm].) Remember to adjust the width measurements of the ground patterns for the Frog Pond (see page 25) and Blossom Bunny (see page 35) collections and any ribbon or rickrack trims accordingly to ensure that they are sewn within the necessary seam allowances.

1 Refer to the individual project instructions to cut the pillow backing and complete the front of the pillow. (The instructions for the pillow fronts are basically the same as for the quilt blocks. Therefore, to avoid unnecessary repetition in the pillow instructions, I will reference the quilt project in that chapter to complete the pillow front.)

2 Pin the two pillow pieces right sides together. Sew around the edges of the pillow using a ¼" (6mm) seam allowance. Be sure to leave an opening large enough at the bottom to insert the pillow form (or stuff with fiberfill).

3 Clip the seam allowance at the corners, turn the pillow right side out and press.

4 Insert the pillow form or stuff firmly with polyester fiberfill. Slip stitch the opening closed. (If using a pillow insert, you can also add small pieces of fiberfill to fill out and add firmness to the sides and corner edges. This may be necessary as pillow inserts can sometimes vary in thickness among different manufacturers. Remember that fiberfill is always an option if you are uncertain about the fit of any pillow insert.)

general instructions: chenille wall hangings

These projects are featured in three basic sizes: 24" × 24" (61cm × 61cm), 22" × 22" (56cm × 56cm) and 18" × 18" (46cm × 46cm).

1 Refer to the individual project instructions to cut the backing and batting and complete the front of the wall hanging. The square piece of batting is generally cut 1" (3cm) smaller due to the unfinished edges of the wall hangings.
Note: To avoid unnecessary repetition for some of these instructions, I reference the quilt project from that same collection.

2 Baste the batting in between the top and bottom layers with the wrong sides of the chenille top and backing facing together. Smooth out any wrinkles in the chenille fabric and batting. Pin the three layers together.

3 Stitch around the edges of the wall hanging and around each of the four chenille squares using a ¼–⅜" (6–10mm) seam allowance. (You will be stitching through the three layers, which will give a quilted effect.)

4 Trim the raw edges even as necessary.

5 If desired, add decorative stitching, such as a running stitch, along the seams of the four chenille corners using four strands of the desired color floss.
Note: I added decorative stitching to only some of the designs.

6 Stitch two plastic loops along the top for hanging, or add a hanging sleeve.

≈✿ Tip: The unfinished edges of the chenille add to the charm of these whimsical wall hangings. However, if you want a more finished edge, simply trim any stray threads or fibers with sharp scissors and spray the edges with a fray preventative.

Baby Shower Idea

Share some love and laughter by making a group baby shower keepsake quilt. The themed block designs of the quilts in this book make it "sew" easy to do since each block can be made separately. Or, plan a few evenings of girly fun with a stitching party to sew your individual blocks in the company of family and friends. If other shower guests want to join the fun, have them contribute by completing the piecing or the binding. Or they can create some matching pillows, bibs or a cuddly fleece blanket for the ultimate gift collection.

Here are some handy tips and ideas for creating your keepsake quilt:

- Designate one person to do the actual purchasing of all the fabric and trims. Not only will you achieve a more coordinated look, but you will also save money by eliminating the need for each person to purchase separate yardage. The fabric and trims for each block and the binding and backing material can then be cut, packaged and distributed to each gal, just like a ready-made quilt kit.

- Remember to specify that the individual blocks be returned by a certain date to allow plenty of time to piece, assemble and bind the quilt.

- Make your keepsake gift even more memorable by having everyone stitch (or sign) their names and the date onto a handmade quilt label. Or package the quilt with a beautiful satin bow and attach a hand-stitched gift tag with the contributor names and completion date.

- Create a keepsake quilt journal for mom and baby featuring photos and personal sentiments of the contributors making the quilt in various stages of completion. Be sure to take a photo of the quilt with mom and baby to add a "happily ever after" chapter to your quilting story.

- Show off your wonderful creation by displaying the quilt at the baby shower. For a creative décor idea, hang a rope for an indoor clothesline, then attach the quilt and any other gifts, such as bibs, blankets, booties, clothing and diapers, using clothespins. Assemble the other wrapped gifts in a laundry basket displayed by the clothesline.

FROG POND

Roll up your pant legs and hop into a room filled with frog pond fun! Complete with fanciful frogs, dreamy dragonflies and fresh-picked blossoms, this cheery collection of decorating delights will make a big splash in the bedroom or nursery. Even the tiniest tadpoles can join in the fun with a cute-as-can-be coordinating baby bib.

frog pond quilt

fabric

COTTON PRINTS

Two 14" × 14" (36cm × 36cm) squares of yellow gingham

10½" × 14" (27cm × 36cm) piece of yellow and white stripe print

Two 7" × 16" (18cm × 41cm) pieces of green print (ground pieces)

Sixteen 5" × 5" (13cm × 13cm) squares of assorted yellow and green prints
Note: I use the same combination of eight prints for the two patchwork blocks.

Scraps of green dot print (dragonfly's wings, spots on frogs and flower centers) and green, white and yellow plaid print (flower centers)

½ yard (½m) green print (border)

½ yard (½m) yellow print (binding)

1⅝ yards (1⅔m) of any color fabric (backing and hanging sleeve)

CHENILLE

Two 9" × 14" (23cm × 36cm) pieces and two 5" × 5" (13cm × 13cm) squares of white chenille

Note: You can substitute another fabric if chenille is not available.

WOOL FELT

Two 12" × 12" (30cm × 30cm) pieces of green felt (frogs)

Scraps of brown and tan felt (cattails), yellow felt (large flowers, small flowers and dots on dragonfly's wings), white felt (frog's eyes, medium flowers and dragonfly's body), green felt (leaves) and black felt (frog's pupils)

supplies

1⅓ (1¼m) yards quilt batting, 45" (114cm) wide

28" (72cm) jumbo white rickrack

14" (36cm) jumbo green rickrack

DMC cotton embroidery floss: white, #310 (black), #3364 (green) and #727 (yellow)

Regular or lightweight paper-backed fusible web

Two ½" (13mm) yellow buttons, two ½" (13mm) white buttons, two ⅜" (10mm) white buttons and a ¼" (6mm) yellow button

Materials and Tools (pages 8–10)

Pattern insert

Be sure to read the Techniques section and the individual project instructions thoroughly before you begin. Use two strands of embroidery floss for all stitching unless otherwise stated.

1 *Prepare the two frog blocks*

Cut two 14" × 14" (36cm × 36cm) squares of yellow gingham.

Referring to the pattern insert, follow the Fusible Web Appliqué instructions on page 13 to fuse the ground pieces onto the bottoms of the 14" × 14" (36cm × 36cm) squares using the green print.

Blanket stitch along the top of the ground pieces with the white floss.

Cut two 14" (36cm) pieces of the jumbo white rickrack. Baste the rickrack onto the two ground pieces, approximately 1½" (4cm) from the bottom. Stitch to secure.

Referring to the pattern insert, trace and cut two frogs from the green felt, two medium flowers and four eyes from the white felt, four pupils from the black felt, four cattail stems from the tan felt and four cattail tops from the brown felt.

Follow the Fusible Web Appliqué instructions to fuse six frog spots using the green dot fabric and two circular flower centers using the green, white and yellow plaid fabric.

Referring to the project photo and pattern for placement, baste the frog pieces, cattails and flowers onto the fabric squares. Remember to reverse the placement of the pieces on the bottom block.

Blanket stitch around the frogs with the white floss, around the frog spots with the yellow floss and around the eyes with the black floss. Add a white running stitch around the pupils. Trace, then backstitch the mouth with the black floss. Stitch a French knot at each end of the mouth. Add the nostrils with the black floss using a satin stitch.

Blanket stitch around the top of the cattails with the white floss. Add a black running stitch along each side of the stem.

Blanket stitch around the flowers with the green floss and around the flower centers with the yellow floss.

Sew a ½" (13mm) yellow button onto each flower center.

2 *Prepare the two patchwork blocks*

Cut sixteen 5" × 5" (13cm × 13cm) squares of the assorted prints.

Cut two 5" × 5" (13cm × 13cm) squares of white chenille for the center blocks.

Referring to the pattern insert, trace and cut two small flowers from the yellow felt.

Follow the Fusible Web Appliqué instructions to fuse two circular flower centers using the green dot fabric.

Baste the flowers onto the center of the chenille squares.

Blanket stitch around the flowers with the green floss and around the circular centers with the white floss.

Sew a ⅜" (10mm) white button onto the center of each flower.

Lay the squares out for each block as desired, with the chenille flower square in the center of the three rows. (Use the project photo as a guide.) Sew the patchwork squares together, connecting the squares for each row first, then sewing the rows together.

3 *Prepare the dragonfly block*

Cut a 10½" × 14" (27cm × 36cm) piece of the yellow and white stripe print.

Referring to the pattern insert, trace and cut the dragonfly body from the white felt and four spots from the yellow felt.

Follow the Fusible Web Appliqué instructions to fuse dragonfly wings at a slight angle to the fabric square, using the green dot fabric.

Referring to the project photo and pattern insert for placement, baste the felt body and four dots onto the wings.

Blanket stitch around the dragonfly's wings with the yellow floss and around the body with the green floss. Add a black running stitch for the antennas and the curlicue underneath. Add two black French knots for the eyes and four green cross stitches, one onto each dot.

Sew a ¼" (6cm) yellow button onto the dragonfly for the nose.

4 *Prepare the two flower blocks*

Cut two 9" × 14" (23cm × 36cm) pieces of white chenille.

Referring to the pattern insert, trace and cut two large flowers from the yellow felt and four leaves from the green felt.

Follow the Fusible Web Appliqué instructions to fuse two circular flower centers using the green dot fabric.

Cut two 7" (18cm) pieces of the jumbo green rickrack for the flower stems. Baste each of the rickrack pieces to the chenille, beginning from the bottom center. Secure them with a running stitch using the green floss (or you can machine stitch if desired).

Referring to the project photo for placement, baste the flowers so that they overlap the tops of the rickrack stems. Baste the leaves, one onto each side of the rickrack stem. (Note that the position of the leaves is reversed on each chenille piece.)

Blanket stitch around the flowers with the green floss and around the circular centers with the white floss. Straight stitch around the leaves with the white floss, then add three running stitches along the center.

Sew a ½" (13mm) white button onto the center of each flower.

5 *Complete the quilt*

Refer to the General Instructions on page 16 to:

Piece the quilt top.

Add the border.

Assemble the layers.

Add a hanging sleeve.
Note: The hanging sleeve can be added after the binding if that is your preferred technique.

Add the binding.

Baby Shower Idea

A Frog Pond baby shower theme is perfect for parents who are decorating their nursery in a gender-neutral yellow or green color scheme. Look for frog- and bug-themed party decorations, tabletop accessories and favors.

frog pond patchwork pillow

fabric

COTTON PRINTS

Eight 5" × 5" (13cm × 13cm) squares of assorted yellow and green prints

14" × 14" (36cm × 36cm) square of any color print (backing)

Scrap of green dot print (flower center)

CHENILLE

5" × 5" (13cm × 13cm) square of yellow chenille (Use white chenille if you want to match the block on the quilt.)

Note: You can substitute another fabric if chenille is not available.

WOOL FELT

Scrap of white felt (small flower)

Note: Use yellow felt if you want to match the block on the quilt.

supplies

14" (36cm) square pillow form (or polyester fiberfill)

DMC cotton embroidery floss: white and #3364 (green)

Regular or lightweight paper-backed fusible web

½" (13mm) yellow button (Use a ⅜" [10mm] white button if you want to match the block on the quilt.)

Materials and Tools (pages 8–10)

Pattern insert

Be sure to read the Techniques section and the individual project instructions thoroughly before you begin. Use two strands of embroidery floss for all stitching unless otherwise stated.

1 Cut a 14" × 14" (36cm × 36cm) square of the backing fabric.

2 Refer to the quilt instructions to make a patchwork flower block for the pillow front, using the eight fabric squares and the chenille square for the center. **Note:** I chose to vary the color of the chenille square and felt flower, but you can finish it to match the quilt exactly if you prefer.

3 Refer to the General Instructions on page 18 to finish the pillow.

frog pond pillow

fabric

COTTON PRINTS

Two 14" × 14" (36cm × 36cm) squares of yellow gingham

7" × 16" (18cm × 41cm) piece of green print (ground)

Scraps of green dot print (spots on frog) and green, white and yellow plaid print (flower center)

WOOL FELT

12" × 12" (30cm × 30cm) square of green felt (frog)

Scraps of brown and tan felt (cattails), white felt (frog's eyes and medium flower) and black felt (frog's pupils)

supplies

14" (36cm) square pillow form (or polyester fiberfill)

14" (36cm) jumbo white rickrack

DMC cotton embroidery floss: white, #310 (black), #3364 (green) and #727 (yellow)

Regular or lightweight paper-backed fusible web

½" (13mm) yellow button

Materials and Tools (page 8–10)

Pattern insert

Be sure to read the Techniques section and the individual project instructions thoroughly before you begin. Use two strands of embroidery floss for all stitching unless otherwise stated.

1 Cut two 14" × 14" (36cm × 36cm) squares of the yellow gingham.

2 Refer to the quilt instructions to make a frog block for the pillow front using a 14" × 14" (36cm × 36cm) fabric square. You will use the other square for the pillow backing.

3 Refer to the General Instructions on page 18 to finish the pillow.

frog pond bib

fabric
|||||||||||||||||||||||||||||||||||||

COTTON PRINTS

⅜ yard (½m) yellow dot print

Scraps of green dot print (frog), white fabric (eyes) and black fabric (pupils)

supplies
|||||||||||||||||||||||||||||||||||||

12" × 12" (30cm × 30cm) square of quilt batting

DMC cotton embroidery floss: white and #310 (black)

Regular or lightweight paper-backed fusible web

30" (76cm) of ¼" (6mm) wide white double-folded bias tape

Materials and Tools (pages 8–10)

Pattern insert

Be sure to read the Techniques section and the individual project instructions thoroughly before you begin. Use two strands of embroidery floss for all stitching unless otherwise stated.

1 Referring to the pattern insert, trace and cut two bib shapes from the yellow dot print and one bib shape from the batting.

2 Follow the Fusible Web Appliqué instructions on page 13 to fuse a frog onto one of the bib pieces (aligning the raw edges along the bottom). Fuse the eyes, then the pupils, using the white and black fabrics respectively.

3 Blanket stitch around the frog with the white floss and around the eyes with the black floss. (There is no need to stitch the raw edge.) Add a white running stitch around the pupils. Trace, then backstitch the mouth with the black floss. Stitch a French knot at each end of the mouth. Add the nostrils with the black floss using a satin stitch.

4 With the edges aligned, baste the bib-shaped batting onto the wrong side of the back fabric bib piece.

5 Pin the two bib pieces right sides together. Sew around the edges of the bib using a ¼" (6mm) seam allowance, leaving the neck area open for turning.

6 Clip the curves of the seam allowance. Turn the bib right side out and press.

7 Close the neck opening with a zigzag stitch.

8 Cut a 30" (76cm) piece of bias tape. Line up the center of the bias tape and the center of the neck opening, then baste the tape into position. There should be equal lengths of the bias tape on each side of the bib.

9 Trim the ends to the desired length. Stitch the bias tape from end to end, catching the bib around the neck area. Knot the ends if desired.

frog pond chenille wall hanging

fabric

COTTON PRINTS

Scraps of green dot print (spots on frog) and green, white and yellow plaid print (flower centers)

CHENILLE

Two 24" × 24" (61cm × 61cm) squares of white chenille

Four 5" × 5" (13cm × 13cm) squares and one 14" × 14" (36cm × 36cm) square of yellow chenille

7" × 16" (18cm × 41cm) piece of pastel green chenille (ground)

WOOL FELT

12" × 12" (30cm × 30cm) square of green felt (frog)

Scraps of brown and tan felt (cattails), white felt (frog's eyes and medium flowers) and black felt (frog's pupils)

supplies

23" × 23" (58cm × 58cm) square of quilt batting

DMC cotton embroidery floss: white, #310 (black), #3364 (green) and #727 (yellow)

Regular or lightweight paper-backed fusible web

Five ½" (13mm) yellow buttons

Two 1" (3cm) plastic loops (for hanging)

Materials and Tools (pages 8–10)

Pattern insert

Be sure to read the Techniques section and the individual project instructions thoroughly before you begin. Use two strands of embroidery floss for all stitching unless otherwise stated.

1 Cut two 24" × 24" (61cm × 61cm) squares of white chenille. Cut a 14" × 14" (36cm × 36cm) square and four 5" × 5" (13cm × 13cm) squares of the yellow chenille. Referring to the pattern insert, trace and cut the ground piece from the pastel green chenille.

2 Cut a 23" × 23" (58cm × 58cm) square of the quilt batting.
Note: Due to the unfinished edges, the batting should be approximately 1" (3cm) less in total size compared to the chenille squares.

3 Referring to the pattern insert, trace and cut a frog from the green felt, five medium flowers and two eyes from the white felt, two pupils from the black felt, two cattail stems from the tan felt and two cattail tops from the brown felt.

4 Follow the Fusible Web Appliqué instructions on page 13 to fuse three frog spots using the green dot print and five circular flower centers using the plaid print.

5 Baste the 14" × 14" (36cm × 36cm) yellow chenille square onto the center of a white chenille square. There should be 5" (13cm) on each side of the square. Baste the green chenille ground piece onto the bottom of the yellow chenille square.

6 Blanket stitch around the green chenille ground piece with four strands of the white floss and around the yellow chenille square with four strands of the green floss.

7 Referring to the project photo and pattern insert for placement, baste the frog pieces, cattails and flower onto the yellow chenille square.

8 Refer to the quilt instructions for the frog blocks to embroider and add the button trim.

9 Baste the four 5" × 5" (13cm × 13cm) yellow chenille squares, one onto each corner. Baste the four remaining flowers onto the centers of the four squares. Embroider and add buttons as described in the quilt instructions for the frog blocks.

10 Refer to the General Instructions on page 18 to complete the wall hanging.

BLOSSOM BUNNY

Sweet bunnies and blossoms add a touch of springtime whimsy to this pretty-in-pink collection. Adorned with delicate embroidery and floral trims, this enchanting bunny theme is the perfect way to add some sugar-'n-spice to the nursery. A fun fleece blanket with playful polka dots makes an adorable shower gift for the snuggle bunny on your list.

blossom bunny quilt

fabric

COTTON PRINTS

Three 14" × 14" (36cm × 36cm) squares of assorted pink prints (or you can use the same pink print for all three blocks)

Three 7" × 16" (18cm × 41cm) pieces of green floral print (ground pieces)

Twenty-four 5" × 5" (13cm × 13cm) squares of assorted pink and green prints
Note: I use the same combination of eight prints for the three patchwork blocks.

Assorted scraps of pink prints (small flowers) and pale green prints (inner ears and flower centers)

½ yard (½m) of green print (border)

½ yard (½m) of pink print (binding)

1⅝ yards (1½m) pink print (backing and hanging sleeve)

CHENILLE

Three 5" × 5" (13cm × 13cm) squares of white chenille
Note: You can substitute another fabric if chenille is not available.

WOOL FELT

Three 11" × 13" (28cm × 33cm) pieces of white felt (bunnies)

Scraps of pink felt (medium flowers), white felt (flower centers) and pastel green felt (leaves)

supplies

1⅓ (1¼m) yards quilt batting, 45" (114cm) wide

42" (107cm) jumbo white rickrack

DMC cotton embroidery floss: white, #604 (pink) and #3053 (green)

Regular or lightweight paper-backed fusible web

Three ¾" (19mm) pink buttons and three ⅜" (10mm) white buttons

Six ¾"(19mm) pink ribbon flowers

Pink blush and cotton swab

Materials and Tools (pages 8–10)

Pattern insert

Be sure to read the Techniques section and the individual project instructions thoroughly before you begin. Use two strands of embroidery floss for all stitching unless otherwise stated.

1 *Prepare the three bunny blocks*

Cut three 14" × 14" (36cm × 36cm) squares of the assorted pink prints (or three squares of the same print).

Referring to the pattern insert, follow the Fusible Web Appliqué instructions on page 13 to fuse three ground pieces onto the bottoms of the 14" × 14" (36cm × 36cm) squares using the green floral print.

Blanket stitch along the top of the ground pieces with the white floss.

Cut three 14" (36cm) pieces of jumbo white rickrack. Baste the rickrack onto the three ground pieces, approximately 1¼" (3cm) from the bottom. Stitch to secure.

Referring to the pattern insert, trace and cut three bunnies and three circular flower centers from the white felt, three medium flowers from the pink felt and six leaves from the pastel green felt.

Follow the Fusible Web Appliqué instructions to fuse six inner ear pieces using the pale green prints.

Referring to the project photo for placement, baste the bunny pieces, leaves and flowers onto the three fabric squares. Vary the placement of the motifs on each block as shown in the photo.

Blanket stitch around the bunnies with the pink floss and around the inner ears with the white floss. The eyes are two green French knots. Sew a pink button for the nose onto each bunny, directly underneath the eyes. Backstitch a small line from the center of the nose with the pink floss.

Blanket stitch around the flowers with the green floss. Add a pink running stitch around the circular flower centers. Straight stitch around the leaves with white, then add three running stitches along the center of each leaf.

Add the decorative flower stems using a running stitch and the green floss. The curlicue leaves are backstitched in green. Stitch the pink ribbon flowers onto the top of each stem.

Apply blush to bunnies' cheeks using a cotton swab.

2 *Prepare the three patchwork blocks*

Cut twenty-four 5" × 5" (13cm x 13cm) squares of the assorted prints.

Cut three 5 × 5" (13cm × 13cm) squares of white chenille for the center blocks.

Follow the Fusible Web Appliqué instructions to fuse three small flowers onto the centers of the chenille blocks using the assorted pink prints. Fuse three flower centers onto the flowers using the pale green print.

Blanket stitch around the flowers with the green floss and around the flower centers with the white floss.

Sew a white button onto the center of each flower.

Lay out the squares for each block as desired, with the flower square in the center of the three rows. (Use the project photo as a guide.) Sew the patchwork squares together.

3 Complete the quilt

Refer to the General Instructions on pages 16 to:

Piece the quilt top.

Add the border.

Assemble the layers.

Add a hanging sleeve.
Note: The hanging sleeve can be added after the binding if that is your preferred technique.

Add the binding.

Sweet Idea

It's "sew" easy to whip up this smaller variation of the Blossom Bunny Quilt.

Simply refer to the quilt instructions to make your 14" × 14" (36cm × 36cm) bunny block. Then cut sixteen 5" × 5" (13cm × 13cm) squares of coordinating fabric to make a charming patchwork border. Sew the squares around the center block to piece your quilt top, then finish according to the general quilting instructions (altering your measurements as necessary).

blossom bunny pillow

fabric

COTTON PRINTS

Two 14" × 14" (36cm × 36cm)
squares of pink dot print

7" × 16" (18cm × 41cm) piece of
green floral print (ground)

Scraps of pale green dot print (inner ears)

WOOL FELT

11" × 13" (28cm × 33cm) piece of white
felt (bunny and flower center)

Scrap of pink felt (medium flower)
and pastel green felt (leaves)

supplies

14" (36cm) square pillow form
(or polyester fiberfill)

14" (36cm) jumbo white rickrack

DMC cotton embroidery floss: white,
#604 (pink) and #3053 (green)

Regular or lightweight paper-backed fusible web

¾" (19mm) pink button

¾" (19mm) pink ribbon flower

Pink blush and cotton swab

Materials and Tools (pages 8–10)

Pattern insert

*Be sure to read the Techniques section
and the individual project instructions
thoroughly before you begin. Use two
strands of embroidery floss for all stitching
unless otherwise stated.*

1 Cut two 14" × 14" (36cm x 36cm)
squares of the pink dot print.

2 Refer to the quilt instructions to
make a bunny block for the pillow front
using a 14" × 14" (36cm × 36cm) fabric
square. You will use the other square for
the pillow backing.

3 Refer to the General Instructions on
page 18 to finish the pillow.

blossom bunny blanket

fabric

COTTON PRINTS

Scraps of pale green stripe print (inner ears) and pink dot print (nose)

FLEECE

Two 30" × 36" (76cm × 91cm) pieces of pink dot or solid pink fleece

Note: I use 1 yard (1m) of 60" (152cm) wide fleece cut in half, so the pieces may be slightly smaller to allow for selvage.

9" × 30" (23cm × 76cm) piece of pastel green fleece (ground)

11" × 13" (28cm × 33cm) piece of white fleece (bunny and flower center)

Scrap of pale pink fleece (medium flower) and pastel green fleece (leaves)

supplies

30" (76cm) jumbo white rickrack

DMC cotton embroidery floss: white, #604 (pink) and #3053 (green)

Regular or lightweight paper-backed fusible web

Materials and Tools (pages 8–10)

Pattern insert

Be sure to read the Techniques section and the individual project instructions thoroughly before you begin. Use two strands of embroidery floss for all stitching unless otherwise stated.

1 Cut two 30" × 36" (76cm × 91cm) pieces of pink dot or solid pink fleece.

2 Cut a 9" × 30" (23cm × 76cm) piece of pastel green fleece for the ground.

3 With the edges aligned, baste the ground piece along the bottom of one of the blanket pieces. Zigzag stitch around the edges to secure.

4 Cut a 30" (76cm) piece of jumbo white rickrack. Baste and stitch the rickrack along the top edge of the ground piece.

5 Referring to the pattern insert, trace and cut a bunny and a circular flower center from the white fleece, a medium flower from the pale pink fleece and two leaves from the pastel green fleece.

6 Follow the Fusible Web Appliqué instructions on page 13 to fuse two inner ear pieces using the pale green stripe print and a nose using the pink dot print.

7 Referring to the project photo for placement, baste the bunny, leaves and flower pieces onto the blanket, overlapping the ground and rickrack trim. The bunny is positioned approximately 6½" (17cm) from the right side.

8 Blanket stitch around the bunny and the nose with the pink floss and around the inner ear pieces with the white floss. Backstitch a small line from the center of the nose with the pink floss. Add two green French knots for the bunny's eyes.

9 Blanket stitch around the flower with the green floss. Add a pink running stitch around the flower center. Straight stitch around the two leaves with the white floss, then add three running stitches along the center of each leaf.

10 With the edges aligned, pin the two blanket pieces right sides together. Sew around the edges of the blanket using a seam allowance of approximately ⅜" (10mm). Be sure to leave an opening large enough for turning.
Note: Fleece fabric tends to stretch and shift a bit, so I generally use more than a ¼" (6mm) seam allowance.

11 Trim the seam allowance at the corners. Turn the blanket right side out, then stitch the opening closed.

blossom bunny chenille wall hanging

fabric

COTTON PRINTS

Scraps of pale green gingham print (inner ears) and pale green dot print (flower centers)

CHENILLE

Two 24" × 24" (61cm × 61cm) squares of white chenille

14" × 14" (36cm × 36cm) square and four 5" × 5" (13cm × 13cm) squares of pink chenille

7" × 16" (18cm × 41cm) piece of pastel green chenille (ground)

WOOL FELT

11" × 13" (28cm × 33cm) piece of white felt (bunny and flower center)

Scraps of white felt (small flowers), pink felt (medium flower) and pastel green felt (leaves)

supplies

23" × 23" (58cm × 58cm) square of quilt batting

DMC cotton embroidery floss: white, #604 (pink) and #3053 (green)

Regular or lightweight paper-backed fusible web

¾" (19mm) pink button

¾" (19mm) pink ribbon flower

Pink blush and cotton swab

Two 1" (3cm) plastic loops (for hanging)

Materials and Tools (pages 8–10)

Pattern insert

Be sure to read the Techniques section and the individual project instructions thoroughly before you begin. Use two strands of embroidery floss for all stitching unless otherwise stated.

1 Cut two 24" × 24" (61cm × 61cm) squares of white chenille. Cut a 14" × 14" (36cm × 36cm) square and four 5" × 5" (13cm x 13cm) squares of the pink chenille. Referring to the pattern insert, trace and cut the ground piece from the piece of pastel green chenille.

2 Cut a 23" × 23" (58cm × 58cm) square of the quilt batting.
Note: Due to the unfinished edges, the batting should be approximately 1" (3cm) less in total size compared to the chenille squares.

3 Referring to the pattern insert, trace and cut a bunny, four small flowers and a medium flower center from the white felt, a medium flower from the pink felt and two leaves from the green felt.

4 Follow the Fusible Web Appliqué instructions on page 13 to fuse two inner ear pieces using the pale green gingham print and four small flower centers using the pale green dot print.

5 Baste the 14" × 14" (36cm × 36cm) pink chenille square onto the center of a white chenille square. There should be 5" (13cm) on each side of the square. Baste the green chenille ground piece onto the bottom of the pink chenille square.

---

6 Blanket stitch around the green chenille ground piece with four strands of the white floss and around the pink chenille square with four strands of the green floss.

7 Referring to the project photo for placement, baste the bunny, leaves and flower onto the pink chenille center square.

8 Refer to the quilt instructions to embroider and to add cheeks, button nose and a pink ribbon flower.

9 Baste the four 5" × 5" (13cm x 13cm) pink chenille squares, one onto each corner. Baste the four white flowers onto the centers of the four squares. Blanket stitch around the flowers with the pink floss and around the flower centers with the white.

10 Refer to the General Instructions on page 18 to complete the wall hanging.

Sweet Idea

Bibs make great baby shower gifts and are the perfect way to use up those excess scraps of fabric. Just follow the general cutting and assembly instructions for the bibs in the Frog Pond and Jungle Chic chapters, and add a cute flower motif and some rickrack trim.

blossom bunny fairy

fabric

COTTON PRINTS

Scraps of pink dot print (inner ears) and lime green print (flower center)

CHENILLE

Two 15" × 22" (38cm × 60cm) pieces of white chenille (bunny)

Two 12" × 19" (30cm × 48cm) pieces of pink chenille (wings)

Scrap of bright pink chenille (large flower)
Note: You can substitute pink felt or use a pink cotton print with fusible web instead of the bright pink chenille.

WOOL FELT

Scraps of lime green felt (leaves)
Note: You can substitute fleece for the lime green felt.

supplies

Polyester fiberfill

DMC cotton embroidery floss: white, #776 (pink) and #907 (lime green)

Regular or lightweight paper-backed fusible web

½" (13mm) pink button and ½" (13mm) white button

10" (25cm) of ⅛" (3mm) wide pink dot ribbon

¾" (19mm) pink ribbon rosebud

6½" (17cm) jumbo lime green rickrack

54" (137cm) white marabou boa trim

Permanent fabric adhesive (such as Fabri-Tac)

Materials and Tools (pages 8–10)

Pattern insert

Be sure to read the Techniques section and the individual project instructions thoroughly before you begin. Use two strands of embroidery floss for all stitching unless otherwise stated.

1 Referring to the pattern insert, trace and cut two bunny pieces from the white chenille, two wing pieces from the pink chenille and a large flower from the bright pink chenille. Trace and cut two leaves from the lime green felt (or fleece).

2 Follow the Fusible Web Appliqué instructions on page 13 to fuse two inner ears onto one of the bunny pieces using the pink dot print. Fuse a large flower center using the lime green print.

3 Blanket stitch around the inner ears with the green floss. Add two green French knots for the eyes. Sew on the pink button for the nose, then backstitch a line approximately 1¼" (3cm) from the center of the nose using four strands of the pink floss.

4 Cut a 6½" (17cm) piece of the jumbo lime green rickrack. Baste it into position onto the center of the bunny, approximately 2" (5cm) from the bottom, for the flower stem. Secure it with a running stitch using the white floss (or you can machine stitch if desired).

5 Baste the chenille flower onto the top of the stem. Baste the two leaves, one onto each side of the stem.

6 Blanket stitch around the flower with four strands of the green floss. Blanket stitch around the flower center with the white floss. Stitch the white button onto the flower center.

7 Straight stitch around the two leaves with the white floss. Then add three running stitches along the center of each leaf.

8 Tie a bow with the 10" (25cm) piece of ⅛" (3mm) wide pink dot ribbon. Stitch the bow and pink rosebud onto the bottom of the rickrack stem.

9 Pin the two bunny pieces wrong sides together. Blanket stitch around the bunny using four strands of the green floss, leaving an opening large enough for stuffing. Stuff the bunny with fiberfill, then blanket stitch the opening closed.

10 Pin the two wing pieces wrong sides together. Sew around the edges of the wings using your preferred stitching technique, leaving an opening large enough for stuffing.
Note: Since the edges of the wings will be concealed with the boa trim, you can use a machine stitch, which will be faster than hand-sewing with a decorative embroidery stitch.

11 Stuff the wings with fiberfill, then stitch the opening closed. Cut a 54" (137cm) piece of the white boa trim. Adhere the boa trim using permanent fabric adhesive.

12 Stitch the wings onto the back of the bunny.

STAR GAZER

Star light, star bright…there's nothing more magical than a starry moonlit night. Little star gazers will adore this dreamy baby-blue collection featuring sweet giraffes, twinkling stars and enchanting moon motifs. A cozy fleece blanket keeps baby warm and cozy while drifting into dreamland.

fabric

||||||||||||||||||||||||||||||||||

COTTON PRINTS

Two 8¾" × 14" (22cm × 36cm) pieces of blue, white and yellow stripe print

Sixteen 5" × 5" (13cm × 13cm) squares of assorted blue, brown and yellow prints
Note: I use the same combination of eight prints for the two patchwork blocks.

Scraps of blue print (inner ears and cheek on moon)

½ yard (½m) of brown print (border)

½ yard (½m) of yellow print (binding)

1⅝ yards (1½m) of any color print (backing and hanging sleeve)

CHENILLE

Two 14" × 14" (36cm × 36cm) squares of blue chenille

Two 10" × 10" (25cm × 25cm) squares, two 5" × 5" (13cm × 13cm) squares, and an 11" × 14" (28cm × 36cm) piece of cream chenille

Note: You can substitute another fabric if chenille is not available.

WOOL FELT

Two 12" × 12" (30cm × 30cm) squares of tan felt (giraffes)

11" × 14" (28cm × 36cm) piece of yellow felt (moon)

Scraps of yellow felt (stars), brown felt (spots on giraffes) and blue felt (noses and horns on giraffes)

supplies

|||||||||||||||||||||||||||||||||||

1⅓ (1¼m) yards quilt batting, 45" (114cm) wide

DMC cotton embroidery floss: ecru, #727 (yellow), #838 (brown) and #157 (blue)

Regular or lightweight paper-backed fusible web

Nine ½" (13mm) pale blue buttons and a ⅜" (10mm) ivory button

Materials and Tools (pages 8–10)

Pattern insert

Be sure to read the Techniques section and the individual project instructions thoroughly before you begin. Use two strands of embroidery floss for all stitching unless otherwise stated.

1 *Prepare the two giraffe blocks*

Cut two 14" × 14" (36cm x 36cm) squares of the blue chenille.

Cut two 10" × 10" (25cm x 25cm) squares of the cream chenille.

Referring to the pattern insert, trace and cut two giraffes from the tan felt, six giraffe spots from the brown felt, two noses and four horns from the blue felt and two stars from the yellow felt. Remember to cut a giraffe and three spots in reverse so they will be facing the opposite direction.

Follow the Fusible Web Appliqué instructions on page 13 to fuse four inner ear pieces using the blue print.

Baste the cream chenille squares onto the center of the blue chenille squares.

Referring to the project photo and pattern insert for placement, baste the giraffe pieces (with the straight edges aligned), one onto the lower left corner and one onto the lower right corner of the cream chenille squares.

Blanket stitch around the cream chenille squares with four strands of the brown floss.

Blanket stitch around the giraffes with the blue floss, around the spots with the ecru floss and around the inner ear pieces with the brown floss. The eyes are two brown French knots. Straight stitch around the noses and horns with the yellow floss.

Referring to the photo for placement, baste the two stars, one overlapping the top right corner and the other overlapping the top left corner. Add a brown running stitch around the edges of each star.

Sew a ½" (13mm) blue button onto the center of each star.

2 *Prepare the two patchwork blocks*

Cut sixteen 5" × 5" (13cm × 13cm) squares of the assorted prints.

Cut two 5" × 5" (13cm × 13cm) squares of cream chenille.

Trace and cut two stars from the yellow felt.

Baste the stars at an angle (facing opposite directions) onto the center of the chenille squares.

Add a brown running stitch around the edges of each star.

Sew a ½" (13mm) blue button onto the center of each star.

Lay the squares out for each block as desired, with the chenille star square in the center (use the photo as a guide). Sew the patchwork squares together.

3 *Prepare the moon block*

Cut an 11" × 14" (28cm × 36cm) piece of cream chenille.

Referring to the pattern insert, trace and cut a moon from the yellow felt.

Follow the Fusible Web Appliqué instructions to fuse the cheek circle onto the moon using the blue print.

Baste the moon onto the center of the chenille background.

Blanket stitch around the moon with the blue floss and around the cheek with the brown floss. The eye is a brown French knot.

Sew the ⅜" (10mm) ivory button onto the cheek.

4 *Prepare the two star blocks*

Cut two 8¾" × 14" (22cm × 36cm) pieces of the blue, white and yellow stripe print.

Referring to the pattern insert, trace and cut five stars from the yellow felt.

Referring to the photo for placement, baste the stars onto the fabric pieces, with three stars on one piece and two on the other.

Add a brown running stitch around the edges of each star.

Sew a ½" (13mm) blue button onto the center of each star.

5 *Complete the quilt*

Refer to the General Instructions on page 16 to:

Piece the quilt top.

Add the border.

Assemble the layers.

Add a hanging sleeve.
Note: The hanging sleeve can be added after the binding if that is your preferred technique.

Add the binding.

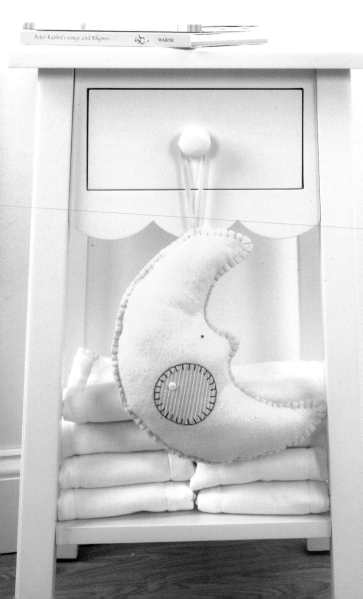

Sweet Idea

This cute felt moon accent looks darling hanging from a doorknob or sitting on a shelf. Simply cut two moon shapes from the wool felt. Embellish one of the moon pieces according to the project instructions. Blanket stitch the wrong sides together, leaving a space for stuffing with fiberfill. Once stuffed, blanket stitch the opening closed. Add a ribbon for hanging onto the back or sandwich the ribbon hanger in between the two felt pieces as you are blanket stitching around the edges.

star gazer patchwork pillow

fabric

COTTON PRINTS

Eight 5" × 5" (13cm × 13cm) squares of assorted blue, brown and yellow prints

14" × 14" (36cm × 36cm) square of any color print (backing)

CHENILLE

5" × 5" (13cm × 13cm) square of cream chenille

Note: You can substitute another fabric if chenille is not available.

WOOL FELT

Scrap of yellow felt (star)

supplies

14" (36cm) square pillow form (or polyester fiberfill)

DMC cotton embroidery floss: #838 (brown)

½" (13mm) pale blue button

Materials and Tools (pages 8–10)

Pattern insert

Be sure to read the Techniques section and the individual project instructions thoroughly before you begin. Use two strands of embroidery floss for all stitching unless otherwise stated.

1 Cut a 14" × 14" (36cm × 36cm) square of the backing fabric.

2 Refer to the quilt instructions to make a patchwork star block for the pillow front, using the eight fabric squares and the chenille square for the center.

3 Refer to the General Instructions on page 18 to finish the pillow.

star gazer chenille wall hanging

fabric

COTTON PRINTS

Scraps of blue print (inner ears)

CHENILLE

Two 18" × 18" (46cm × 46cm) squares of blue chenille

10" × 10" (25cm × 25cm) square and four 4" × 4" (10cm × 10cm) squares of cream chenille

WOOL FELT

12" × 12" (30cm × 30cm) square of tan felt (giraffe)

Scraps of yellow felt (stars), brown felt (spots on giraffe) and blue felt (nose and horns on giraffe)

supplies

17" × 17" (43cm × 43cm) square of quilt batting

DMC cotton embroidery floss: ecru, #727 (yellow), #838 (brown) and #157 (blue)

Regular or lightweight paper-backed fusible web

Three ½" (13mm) pale blue buttons

Two 1" (3cm) plastic loops (for hanging)

Materials and Tools (pages 8–10)

Pattern insert

Be sure to read the Techniques section and the individual project instructions thoroughly before you begin. Use two strands of embroidery floss for all stitching unless otherwise stated.

1 Cut two 18" × 18" (46cm × 46cm) squares of blue chenille. Cut a 10" × 10" (25cm × 25cm) square and four 4" × 4" (10cm × 10cm) squares of the cream chenille.

2 Cut a 17" × 17" (43cm × 43cm) square of the quilt batting.
Note: Due to the unfinished edges, the batting should be approximately 1" (3cm) less in total size compared to the chenille squares.

3 Referring to the pattern insert, trace and cut a giraffe from the tan felt, three spots from the brown felt, a nose and two horns from the blue felt and three stars from the yellow felt.

4 Follow the Fusible Web Appliqué instructions on page 13 to fuse two inner ear pieces using the blue print.

5 Baste the 10" × 10" (25cm × 25cm) cream chenille square onto the center of a blue chenille square. There should be 4" (10cm) on each side of the square.

6 Referring to the project photo and pattern insert for placement, baste the giraffe pieces, with the straight edges aligned, onto the lower left corner of the cream chenille square.

7 Blanket stitch around the cream chenille square with four strands of the brown floss. Refer to the quilt instructions for the giraffe block to embroider the giraffe pieces.

8 Baste the three stars. Embroider and add buttons as described in the quilt instructions for the giraffe or star blocks.

9 Baste the four 4" (10cm) cream chenille squares, one onto each corner.

10 Refer to the General Instructions on page 18 to complete the wall hanging. If desired, add a decorative running stitch around the four corners using four strands of the brown floss.

Decorating Tip

You can create inexpensive wall art by framing a special memory! Start by purchasing a variety of picture frames at your local dollar store. For the nursery, frame the newborn's handprint or footprint at birth, three months, six months, etc. For toddlers, frame their precious artwork. Use shadow boxes to display three-dimensional keepsake items. Or you can use photo transfer paper to add digital images onto your fabric to make memory crafts such as pillows and quilts.

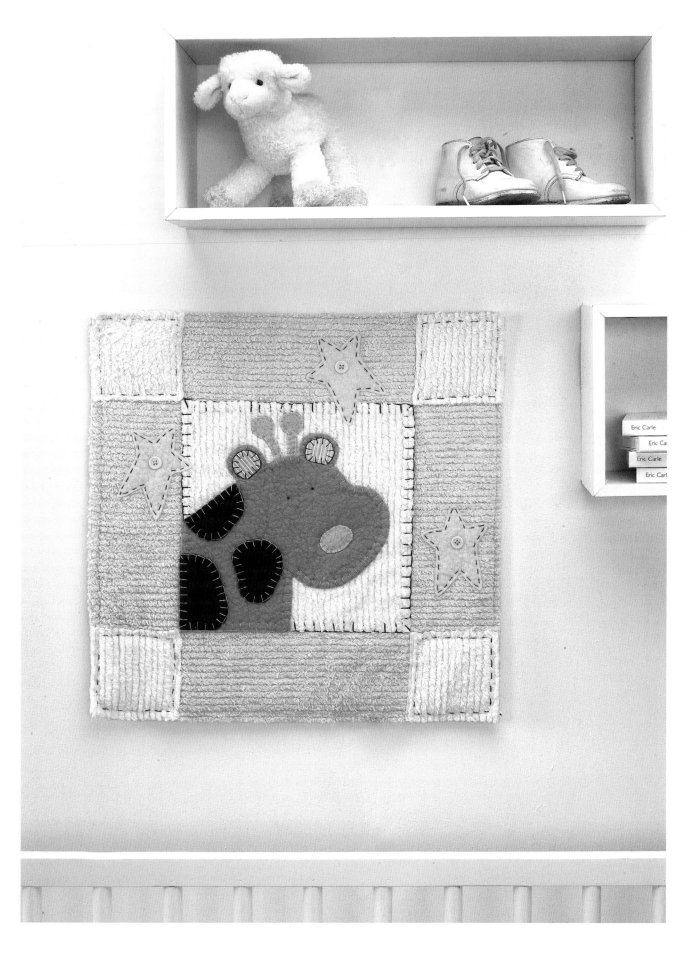

star gazer blanket

fabric

COTTON PRINTS

Scraps of blue print (inner ears)

FLEECE

Two 30" × 36" (76cm × 91cm) pieces of blue dot or solid blue fleece

Note: I use 1 yard (1m) of 60" (152cm) wide fleece cut in half, so the pieces may be slightly smaller to allow for selvage.

10" × 10" (25cm × 25cm) square piece of cream fleece

12" × 12" (30cm × 30cm) square piece of tan fleece (giraffe)

Scraps of yellow fleece (star), brown fleece (spots on giraffe) and blue fleece (nose and horns)

supplies

DMC cotton embroidery floss: ecru, #727 (yellow), #838 (brown) and #157 (blue)

Regular or lightweight paper-backed fusible web

Materials and Tools and (pages 8–10)

Pattern insert

Be sure to read the Techniques section and the individual project instructions thoroughly before you begin. Use two strands of embroidery floss for all stitching unless otherwise stated.

1 Cut two 30" × 36" (76cm × 91cm) pieces of blue dot or solid blue fleece.

2 Cut a 10" × 10" (25cm × 25cm) square of cream fleece.

3 Referring to the pattern insert, trace and cut a giraffe from the tan fleece, three giraffe spots from the brown fleece, a star from the yellow fleece and a nose and two horns from the blue fleece.

4 Follow the Fusible Web Appliqué instructions on page 13 to fuse two inner ear pieces using the blue print.

5 Baste the 10" × 10" (25cm × 25cm) fleece square approximately 6" (15cm) from the right side and 6" (15cm) from the bottom of one of the blanket pieces.

6 Referring to the project photo and pattern insert for placement, baste the giraffe pieces, with the straight edges aligned, onto the lower left corner of the cream fleece square.

7 Blanket stitch around the fleece square with the brown floss.

8 Blanket stitch around the giraffe with the blue floss, around the three spots with the ecru floss and around the inner ears with the brown floss. Straight stitch around the nose and horns with the yellow floss. Add two brown French knots for the giraffe's eyes.

9 Baste the star so that it overlaps the top right edge. Add a brown running stitch around the edges of the star.

10 With the edges aligned, pin the two blanket pieces right sides together. Sew around the edges of the blanket using a seam allowance of approximately ⅜" (10mm). Be sure to leave an opening large enough for turning.
Note: Fleece fabric tends to stretch and shift a bit so I generally use more than a ¼" (6mm) seam allowance.

11 Trim the seam allowance at the corners. Turn the blanket right side out, then stitch the opening closed.

star gazer pillow

fabric
||||||||||||||||||||||||||||||||

COTTON PRINTS
Scraps of blue print (inner ears)

CHENILLE
Two 14" × 14" (36cm × 36cm) squares of blue chenille

10" × 10" (25cm × 25cm) square of cream chenille

Note: You can substitute another fabric if chenille is not available.

WOOL FELT
12" × 12" (30cm × 30cm) square of tan felt (giraffe)

Scraps of yellow felt (star), brown felt (spots on giraffe) and blue felt (nose and horns)

supplies
||||||||||||||||||||||||||||||||

14" (36cm) square pillow form (or polyester fiberfill)

DMC cotton embroidery floss: ecru, #727 (yellow), #838 (brown) and #157 (blue)

Regular or lightweight paper-backed fusible web

½" (13mm) pale blue button

Materials and Tools (pages 8–10)

Pattern insert

Be sure to read the Techniques section and the individual project instructions thoroughly before you begin. Use two strands of embroidery floss for all stitching unless otherwise stated.

1 Cut two 14" × 14" (36cm × 36cm) squares of the blue chenille.

2 Refer to the quilt instructions to make the giraffe block for the pillow front using one of the 14" × 14" (36cm × 36cm) chenille squares. You will use the other square for the pillow backing.

3 Refer to the General Instructions on page 18 to finish the pillow.

Sweet Idea

This charming gift bag is a great way to use leftover scraps of fabric. It makes the perfect baby shower gift when filled with small toys or bath products, and Mom can use the bag to store nursery essentials. Adjust your fabric measurements as necessary to make larger gift bags for quilts and blankets.

Cut two 11" × 18" (28cm × 46cm) pieces of fabric (or cut fabric to your desired size) and decorate the front piece with a star block appliqué, a button and rickrack trim. After stitching your motif, pin the two pieces right sides together and sew along the bottom and two sides, leaving the top side open. To make the casing, fold the top edge over approximately ½" (13mm) and press. Fold the edge again approximately 1" (3cm) and press. Stitch along the top and bottom edges of the casing. Clip the corners, turn and press. Cut a small slit in the center of the casing through the top layer of the fabric only. Cut a piece of ribbon, approximately 40" (102cm) in length. Use a safety pin to string the length of the ribbon through the casing.

Sweet Idea

Bibs make great baby shower gifts and are the perfect way to use up those excess scraps of fabric. Just follow the general cutting and assembly instructions for the bibs in the Frog Pond and Jungle Chic chapters, then add a star motif and some rickrack trim.

 # JUNGLE CHIC

Little kings and queens of the jungle will go ape over this chic safari-inspired collection of designer décor. Whimsical lions, monkeys and giraffes are accented with cozy chenilles and earth tones of green, beige and brown—perfect for decorating a gender-neutral nursery. New moms will love taming their wild ones with a cute lion bib—a wonderful baby shower gift to coordinate with this stylish collection.

jungle chic quilt

fabric

||||||||||||||||||||||||||||||||

COTTON PRINTS

Twenty-four 5" × 5" (13cm × 13cm) squares
of assorted green, brown and tan prints
Note: I use the same combination of eight
prints for the three patchwork blocks.

Scraps of assorted green prints (inner ears)

½ yard (½m) of brown print (border)

½ yard (½m) of green print (binding)

1⅝ yards (1½m) any color print
(backing and hanging sleeve)

CHENILLE

Three 14" × 14" (36cm × 36cm)
squares of pale green chenille

Three 10" × 10" (25cm × 25cm)
squares and three 5" × 5" (13cm ×
13cm) squares of cream chenille

Note: You can substitute another
fabric if chenille is not available.

WOOL FELT

Two 12" × 12" (30cm × 30cm) squares
of tan felt (giraffe and lion's mane)

Scraps of tan felt (monkey's mouth), brown felt
(monkey's head and spots on giraffe), cream
felt (lion's head and monkey's eye piece) and
green felt (noses, letters and horns on giraffe)

supplies

||||||||||||||||||||||||||||||||

1⅓ yards (1¼m) quilt batting, 45" (114cm) wide

DMC cotton embroidery floss: ecru, #838
(brown), #580 (green) and #738 (tan)

Regular or lightweight paper-backed fusible web

Materials and Tools (pages 8–10)

Pattern insert

---

*Be sure to read the Techniques section
and the individual project instructions
thoroughly before you begin. Use two
strands of embroidery floss for all stitching
unless otherwise stated.*

1 *Prepare the giraffe block*

Cut a 14" × 14" (36cm × 36cm) square of
the pale green chenille.

Cut a 10" × 10" (25cm × 25cm) square of
the cream chenille.

Referring to the pattern insert, trace and
cut a giraffe from the tan felt, three giraffe
spots from the brown felt and a nose and
two horns from the green felt.

Follow the Fusible Web Appliqué
instructions on page 13 to fuse two inner
ear pieces using one of the assorted
green prints.

Baste the cream chenille square onto the
center of the green chenille square.

Referring to the project photo and
pattern insert for placement, baste the
giraffe pieces, with the straight edges
aligned, onto the lower left corner of the
cream chenille square.

Blanket stitch around the cream
chenille square with four strands of the
brown floss.

Blanket stitch around the giraffe with
the green floss, around the spots with
the ecru floss and around the inner ear
pieces with the brown floss. The eyes are
two brown French knots. Straight stitch
around the nose and horns with the
ecru floss.

---

2 *Prepare the monkey block*

Cut a 14" × 14" (36cm × 36cm) square of
the pale green chenille.

Cut a 10" × 10" (25cm × 25cm) square of
the cream chenille.

Referring to the pattern insert, trace and
cut a monkey head from the brown felt,
an eye piece from the cream felt, a mouth
piece from the tan felt and a nose from
the green felt.

Follow the Fusible Web Appliqué
instructions to fuse two inner ear pieces
using one of the assorted green prints.

Baste the cream chenille square onto
the center of the green chenille square.
Blanket stitch around the cream
chenille square with four strands of the
brown floss.

Referring to the project photo and
pattern insert for placement, baste the
monkey pieces onto the center of the
cream chenille square.

Blanket stitch around the head with the
ecru floss, around the eye piece with the
brown floss, around the mouth piece
with the green floss and around the inner
ear pieces with the tan floss. The eyes
are two brown French knots. Straight
stitch around the nose with the ecru floss.
Trace, then backstitch the mouth with
the brown floss and the eye accents with
the green.

3 *Prepare the lion block*

Cut a 14" × 14" (36cm × 36cm) square of the pale green chenille.

Cut a 10" × 10" (25cm × 25cm) square of the cream chenille.

Referring to the pattern insert, trace and cut a lion mane from the tan felt, a lion head from the cream felt and a nose from the green felt.

Follow the Fusible Web Appliqué instructions to fuse two inner ear pieces using one of the assorted green prints.

Baste the cream chenille square onto the center of the green chenille square. Blanket stitch around the cream chenille square with four strands of the brown floss.

Referring to the project photo and pattern insert for placement, baste the lion pieces onto the center of the cream chenille square.

Blanket stitch around the mane and inner ear pieces with the green floss and around the head with the brown floss. The eyes are two brown French knots. Straight stitch around the nose with the ecru floss. Trace, then backstitch the mouth with the green floss.

4 *Prepare the three patchwork blocks*

Cut twenty-four 5" × 5" (13cm × 13cm) squares of the assorted prints.
Note: I use the same combination of eight prints for the three blocks.

Cut three 5" × 5" (13cm × 13cm) squares of the cream chenille.

Referring to the pattern insert, trace and cut a G, M and L from the green felt.

Baste the letters onto the centers of the chenille squares.

Blanket stitch around the letters with the ecru floss.

Lay out the squares for each block as desired, with the chenille letter squares in the center. (Use the photo as a guide.) Position the G block to the right of the giraffe, the M block to the left of the monkey and the L block to the right of the lion. Sew the patchwork squares together.

5 *Complete the quilt*

Refer to the General Instructions on page 16 to:

Piece the quilt top.

Add the border.

Assemble the layers.

Add a hanging sleeve.
Note: The hanging sleeve can be added after the binding if that is your preferred technique.

Add the binding.

Baby Shower Ideas

The Jungle Chic collection inspires a "Welcome the Wild One" gender-neutral baby shower. There are oodles of jungle- and safari-themed party items available in just about any color scheme. Or, if you're celebrating the gender of the new arrival, you can easily use a pink monkey theme (Funky Monkeys) for a girl or a blue giraffe theme (Star Gazer) for a boy.

Sweet Idea

Try creating this smaller variation of the Jungle Chic Quilt.

Refer to the quilt instructions to make your 14" × 14" (36cm × 36cm) lion block using wool felt and cotton print backgrounds instead of chenille. You could also use the giraffe or monkey motif if you prefer. Then cut sixteen 5" × 5" (13cm × 13cm) squares of coordinating fabric to make a charming patchwork border. Sew the squares around the center block to piece your quilt top, then finish according to the general quilting instructions, altering your measurements as necessary.

jungle chic chenille wall hanging

fabric

COTTON PRINTS

Scraps of green print (inner ears)

CHENILLE

Two 18" × 18" (46cm × 46cm) squares of pale green chenille

10" × 10" (25cm × 25cm) square and four 4" × 4" (10cm × 10cm) squares of cream chenille

WOOL FELT

Scraps of brown felt (monkey head), tan felt (mouth piece), cream felt (eye piece) and green (nose)

supplies

17" × 17" (43cm × 43cm) square of quilt batting

DMC cotton embroidery floss: ecru, #838 (brown), #580 (green) and #738 (tan)

Regular or lightweight paper-backed fusible web

Two 1" (3cm) plastic loops (for hanging)

Materials and Tools (pages 8–10)

Pattern insert

Be sure to read the Techniques section and the individual project instructions thoroughly before you begin. Use two strands of embroidery floss for all stitching unless otherwise stated.

1 Cut two 18" × 18" (46cm × 46cm) squares of pale green chenille. Cut a 10" × 10" (25cm × 25cm) square and four 4" × 4" (10cm × 10cm) squares of the cream chenille.

2 Cut a 17" × 17" (43cm × 43cm) square of the quilt batting.
Note: Due to the unfinished edges, the batting should be approximately 1" (3cm) less in total size compared to the chenille squares.

3 Referring to the pattern insert, trace and cut a monkey head from the brown felt, an eye piece from the cream felt, a mouth piece from the tan felt and a nose from the green felt.

4 Follow the Fusible Web Appliqué instructions on page 13 to fuse two inner ear pieces using the green print.

5 Baste the 10" × 10" (25cm × 25cm) cream chenille square onto the center of a green chenille square. There should be 4" (10cm) on each side of the square.

6 Blanket stitch around the cream chenille square with four strands of the brown floss.

7 Referring to the project photo and pattern insert for placement, baste the monkey pieces onto the center of the cream chenille square.

8 Refer to the quilt instructions to embroider.

9 Baste the four 4" × 4" (10cm × 10cm) cream chenille squares, one onto each corner.

10 Refer to the General Instructions on page 18 to complete the wall hanging. If desired, add a decorative running stitch around the four corners using four strands of the brown floss.

Decorating Tip

Shop smart. Keep a small notebook with paint and fabric swatches handy so you can refer to them at any time when purchasing your materials, furnishings and accessories. Use the notebook to list product prices you come across in each store to help you with comparison shopping.

jungle chic bib

fabric

COTTON PRINTS

⅜ yard (⅓m) of green print

Scrap of tan plaid print (lion mane)

WOOL FELT

Scraps of cream felt (lion head) and green felt (nose)

supplies

12" × 12" (30cm × 30cm) square of quilt batting

DMC cotton embroidery floss: #838 (brown) and #580 (green)

Regular or lightweight paper-backed fusible web

30" (76cm) of ¼" (6mm) wide white double-folded bias tape

Materials and Tools (pages 8–10)

Pattern insert

Be sure to read the Techniques section and the individual project instructions thoroughly before you begin. Use two strands of embroidery floss for all stitching unless otherwise stated.

1 Referring to the pattern insert, trace and cut two bib shapes from the green print and one bib shape from the batting.

2 Follow the Fusible Web Appliqué instructions on page 13 to fuse the lion's mane using the tan plaid print.

3 Trace and cut a lion's head from the cream felt and a nose from the green felt.

4 Referring to the photo and pattern insert for placement, baste the head and nose onto the bib.

5 Blanket stitch around the mane with the green floss and around the head with the brown floss. Add a green cross stitch onto the center of the nose. The eyes are two brown French knots. Trace, then backstitch the mouth with the green floss.

6 With the edges aligned, baste the bib-shaped batting onto the wrong side of the back fabric bib piece.

7 Pin the two bib pieces right sides together. Sew around the edges of the bib using a ¼" (6mm) seam allowance, leaving the neck area open for turning.

8 Clip the curves of the seam allowance. Turn the bib right side out and press.

9 Close the neck opening with a zigzag stitch.

10 Cut a 30" (76cm) piece of bias tape. Line up the center of the bias tape and the center of the neck opening, then baste the tape into position. There should be equal lengths of the bias tape on each side of the bib.

11 Trim the ends to the desired length. Stitch the bias tape from end to end, catching the bib around the neck area. Knot the ends if desired.

Baby Shower Idea

If the new mom is a sewer, ask guests to use coordinating fabric scraps and trims instead of traditional gift wrap for their baby shower gifts. (To help coordinate the color scheme, include fabric swatch samples that match the nursery in the invitations.) Mom can use the stash of fabrics to make baby-related crafts and nursery décor projects. It's a great way to recycle and think green!

jungle chic giraffe, monkey and lion pillows

fabric
||||||||||||||||||||||||||||||||

COTTON PRINTS

Scraps of assorted green prints (inner ears)

CHENILLE

For each pillow:

Two 14" × 14" (36cm × 36cm) squares of pale green chenille

10" × 10" (25cm × 25cm) square of cream chenille

Note: You can substitute another fabric if chenille is not available.

WOOL FELT

Two 12" × 12" (30cm × 30cm) squares of tan felt (giraffe and lion's mane)

Scraps of tan felt (monkey's mouth), brown felt (monkey's head and spots on giraffe), cream felt (lion's head and monkey's eye piece) and green felt (noses and horns on giraffe)

supplies
||||||||||||||||||||||||||||||||

14" (36cm) square pillow form (or polyester fiberfill) (for each pillow)

DMC cotton embroidery floss: ecru, #838 (brown), #580 (green) and #738 (tan)

Regular or lightweight paper-backed fusible web

Materials and Tools (pages 8–10)

Pattern insert

Be sure to read the Techniques section and the individual project instructions thoroughly before you begin. Use two strands of embroidery floss for all stitching unless otherwise stated.

1 Cut two 14" × 14" (36cm × 36cm) squares of the pale green chenille for each pillow.

2 Refer to the quilt instructions to make the desired block (giraffe, monkey or lion) for the pillow front using a 14" × 14" (36cm × 36cm) chenille square. The other square will be used for the pillow backing.

3 Refer to the General Instructions on page 18 to finish the pillow.

Sweet Idea

Remember that using a chenille fabric in your pillow design is purely optional. The monkey pillow on the bed demonstrates how you can be creative in your fabric choices by using a wool felt and playful cotton print for a completely different twist on the design. You can carry over this same look to the quilt and the other pillows in the collection.

FUNKY MONKEYS

Little fashion monkeys will go bananas over this fresh and funky collection of delectable diva décor. Yummy cupcakes accented with candy-striped ribbon and cotton candy marabou trim lend sweet touches of style to this fabulously feminine theme.

funky monkeys quilt

fabric

COTTON PRINTS

Two 14" × 14" (36cm × 36cm) squares of pink dot print

Two 8¾" × 14" (22cm × 36cm) pieces of dark brown print

Sixteen 5" × 5" (13cm × 13cm) squares of assorted pink and brown prints

Note: I use the same combination of eight prints for the two patchwork blocks.

Scraps of pink and brown print (inner ears)

½ yard (½m) of pink print (border)

½ yard (½m) of brown print (binding)

1⅝ yards (1½m) of any color print (backing and hanging sleeve)

CHENILLE

Two 10" × 10" (25cm × 25cm) squares, two 5" × 5" (13cm × 13cm) squares, and an 11" × 14" (28cm × 36cm) piece of cream chenille

Note: You can substitute another fabric if chenille is not available.

WOOL FELT

Scraps of pink felt (extra-large flowers, cupcake bottom and cherry, hearts, and monkeys' noses), cream felt (monkeys' eye pieces), brown felt (monkeys' heads, cupcake topping and flower cone centers) and tan felt (cones, cupcake top and monkeys' mouth pieces)

supplies

1⅓ yards (1¼m) quilt batting, 45" (114cm) wide

DMC cotton embroidery floss: ecru, #3716 (pink), #838 (brown) and #738 (tan)

Regular or lightweight paper-backed fusible web

5" (13cm) of ⅞" (2cm) wide pink and brown striped ribbon

Seven 1" (3cm) pink ribbon flowers

6" (15cm) pink marabou boa trim

Permanent fabric adhesive (such as Fabri-Tac)

Materials and Tools (pages 8–10)

Pattern insert

Be sure to read the Techniques section and the individual project instructions thoroughly before you begin. Use two strands of embroidery floss for all stitching unless otherwise stated.

1 *Prepare the two monkey blocks*

Cut two 14" × 14" (36cm × 36cm) squares of the pink dot print.

Cut two 10" × 10" (25cm × 25cm) squares of the cream (or white) chenille.

Baste the chenille squares onto the centers of the 14" × 14" (36cm × 36cm) squares. Blanket stitch around the chenille squares with four strands of the brown floss.

Referring to the pattern insert, trace and cut two monkey heads from the brown felt, two eye pieces from the cream felt, two mouth pieces from the tan felt and two noses from the pink felt.

Follow the Fusible Web Appliqué instructions on page 13 to fuse two inner ear pieces onto each felt monkey head using the pink and brown print.

Referring to the project photo and pattern insert for placement, baste the monkey pieces onto the center of the chenille squares.

Blanket stitch around the heads and noses with the ecru floss, around the eye pieces with the brown floss, around the mouth pieces with the pink floss and around the inner ear pieces with the tan floss. The eyes are two brown French knots. Trace, then backstitch the mouths with the brown floss and the eye accents with the pink floss.

2 *Prepare the two patchwork blocks*

Cut sixteen 5" × 5" (13cm × 13cm) squares of the assorted prints.

Cut two 5" × 5" (13cm × 13cm) squares of the cream chenille.

Referring to the pattern insert, trace and cut two hearts from the pink felt, with one in reverse.

Baste the hearts at a slight angle onto the center of the chenille squares.

Blanket stitch around the hearts with the brown floss.

Stitch a pink ribbon flower onto the top center of each heart.

Lay out the squares for each block as desired, with the chenille heart square in the center. (Use the photo as a guide.) Sew the patchwork squares together.

3 *Prepare the cupcake block*

Cut an 11" × 14" (28cm × 36cm) piece of the cream chenille.

Referring to the pattern insert, trace and cut a cupcake bottom and cherry from the pink felt, a cupcake top from the tan felt and a topping piece from the brown felt.

Referring to the photo and pattern insert for placement, baste the cupcake pieces onto the center of the chenille background.

Cut a 5" (13cm) piece of the pink and brown ribbon. Trim the ends of the ribbon at a slight angle so that they align with the edges of the cupcake bottom. Baste and stitch the ribbon piece approximately ⅝" (16mm) from the bottom of the cupcake.

Blanket stitch around the bottom and sides of the cupcake with the brown floss, around the top of the cupcake with pink floss, around the topping with ecru floss and around the cherry with brown floss.

Use permanent fabric adhesive to adhere the pink marabou boa trim onto the cupcake.

Stitch three pink flower trims spaced evenly along the ribbon piece.

4 *Prepare the two flower cone blocks*

Cut two 8¾" × 14" (22cm × 36cm) pieces of the dark brown print.

Referring to the pattern insert, trace and cut two extra-large flowers from the pink felt, two circular flower centers from the brown felt and two cones from the tan felt.

Referring to the photo and pattern insert for placement, baste the flower cone pieces onto the centers of the 8¾" × 14" (22cm × 36cm) pieces.

Blanket stitch around the flowers with brown floss, around the cones with pink floss and around the circular flower centers with ecru floss.

Stitch a pink ribbon flower onto the center of each flower.

5 *Complete the quilt*

Refer to the General Instructions on page 16 to:

Piece the quilt top.

Add the border.

Assemble the layers.

Add a hanging sleeve.
Note: The hanging sleeve can be added after the binding if that is your preferred technique.

Add the binding.

Baby Shower Ideas

Stitch a cuddly fleece baby blanket to coordinate with your themed décor collection. (Use the blankets on pages 36 and 50 as inspiration.) The blanket can be used to decorate the gift table at the baby shower. Or roll up the blanket and tie it with a beautiful satin ribbon, accented with a hand-stitched gift tag.

funky monkeys pillow

fabric

COTTON PRINTS

Two 14" × 14" (36cm × 36cm) squares of pink dot print

Scraps of pink and brown print (inner ears)

CHENILLE

10" × 10" (25cm × 25cm) square of cream chenille

Note: You can substitute another fabric if chenille is not available.

WOOL FELT

Scraps of pink felt (nose), cream felt (eye piece), brown felt (head) and tan felt (mouth piece)

supplies

14" (36cm) square pillow form (or polyester fiberfill)

DMC cotton embroidery floss: ecru, #3716 (pink), #838 (brown) and #738 (tan)

Regular or lightweight paper-backed fusible web

Materials and Tools (pages 8–10)

Pattern insert

Be sure to read the Techniques section and the individual project instructions thoroughly before you begin. Use two strands of embroidery floss for all stitching unless otherwise stated.

1 Cut two 14" × 14" (36cm × 36cm) squares of the pink dot print.

2 Refer to the quilt instructions to make a monkey block for the pillow front using a 14" × 14" (36cm × 36cm) fabric square. You will use the other square for the pillow backing.

3 Refer to the General Instructions on page 18 to finish the pillow.

funky monkeys patchwork pillow

fabric

COTTON PRINTS

Eight 5" × 5" (13cm × 13cm) squares of assorted pink and brown prints

14" × 14" (36cm × 36cm) fabric square (backing)

CHENILLE

5" × 5" (13cm × 13cm) square of cream chenille

Note: You can substitute another fabric if chenille is not available.

WOOL FELT

Scrap of pink felt (heart)

supplies

14" (36cm) square pillow form (or polyester fiberfill)

DMC cotton embroidery floss: #838 (brown)

1" (3cm) pink ribbon flower

Materials and Tools (pages 8–10)

Pattern insert

Be sure to read the Techniques section and the individual project instructions thoroughly before you begin. Use two strands of embroidery floss for all stitching unless otherwise stated.

1 Cut a 14" × 14" (36cm × 36cm) square of the backing fabric.

2 Refer to the quilt instructions to make a patchwork heart block for the pillow front, using the eight fabric squares and the chenille square for the center.

3 Refer to the General Instructions on page 18 to finish the pillow.

funky monkeys cupcake pillow

fabric

CHENILLE

Two 14" × 14" (36cm × 36cm) squares of cream chenille

Note: You can substitute another fabric if chenille is not available.

WOOL FELT

Scraps of pink felt (cupcake bottom and cherry), tan felt (cupcake top) and brown felt (cupcake topping)

supplies

14" (36cm) square pillow form (or polyester fiberfill)

DMC cotton embroidery floss: ecru, #3716 (pink) and #838 (brown)

5" (13cm) ⅞" (3cm) wide pink and brown striped ribbon

Three 1" (3cm) pink ribbon flowers

6" (15cm) pink marabou boa trim

Permanent fabric adhesive (such as Fabri-Tac)

Materials and Tools (pages 8–10)

Pattern insert

Be sure to read the Techniques section and the individual project instructions thoroughly before you begin. Use two strands of embroidery floss for all stitching unless otherwise stated.

1 Cut two 14" × 14" (36cm × 36cm) squares of the cream chenille.

2 Refer to the quilt instructions to make a cupcake block for the pillow front using one of the 14" (36cm) square chenille pieces. You will use the other square for the pillow backing.

3 Refer to the General Instructions on page 18 to finish the pillow.

funky monkeys chenille wall hanging

fabric

COTTON PRINTS

Scraps of pink and brown print (inner ears)

CHENILLE

Two 18" × 18" (46cm × 46cm) squares of bright pink chenille

10" × 10" (25cm × 25cm) square and four 4" × 4" (10cm × 10cm) squares of cream chenille

WOOL FELT

Scraps of pink felt (nose), cream felt (eye piece), brown felt (head) and tan felt (mouth piece)

supplies

17" × 17" (43cm × 43cm) square of quilt batting

DMC cotton embroidery floss: ecru, #3716 (pink), #838 (brown) and #738 (tan)

Regular or lightweight paper-backed fusible web

Two 1" (3cm) plastic loops (for hanging)

Materials and Tools (pages 8–10)

Pattern insert

Be sure to read the Techniques section and the individual project instructions thoroughly before you begin. Use two strands of embroidery floss for all stitching unless otherwise stated.

1 Cut two 18" × 18" (46cm × 46cm) squares of bright pink chenille. Cut a 10" × 10" (25cm × 25cm) square and four 4 × 4" (10cm × 10cm) squares of the cream chenille.

2 Cut a 17" × 17" (43cm × 43cm) square of the quilt batting.
Note: Due to the unfinished edges, the batting should be approximately 1" (3cm) less in total size compared to the chenille squares.

3 Referring to the pattern insert, trace and cut a monkey head from the brown felt, an eye piece from the cream felt, a mouth piece from the tan felt and a nose from the pink felt.

4 Follow the Fusible Web Appliqué instructions on page 13 to fuse two inner ear pieces using the pink and brown print.

5 Baste the 10" × 10" (25cm × 25cm) cream chenille square onto the center of a pink chenille square. There should be 4" (10cm) on each side of the square.

6 Blanket stitch around the cream chenille square with four strands of the brown floss.

7 Referring to the project photo and pattern insert for placement, baste the monkey pieces onto the center of the cream chenille square.

8 Refer to the quilt instructions to embroider.

9 Baste the four 4" × 4" (10cm × 10cm) cream chenille squares, one onto each corner.

10 Refer to the General Instructions on page 18 to complete the wall hanging. If desired, add a decorative running stitch around the four corners using four strands of brown floss.

Decorating Tip

Keep the walls a neutral shade and bring in the color and theme for the child's space with the accessories you choose (such as the projects in this book). This will save you money in the long run since you won't have to keep repainting or wallpapering the room as your child's tastes change. It's much quicker and less expensive to change the accessories.

MANGO TANGO

Bright and bold tangerine elephants and playful polka dots make this sophisticated ensemble the perfect choice for a fresh, modern look. Add some felt flowers, and your safari adventure is complete.

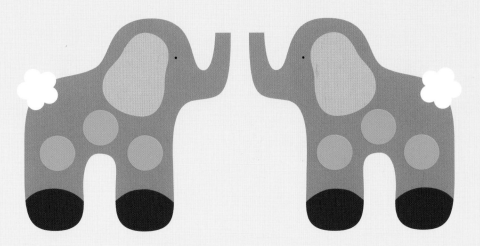

mango tango quilt

fabric

COTTON PRINTS

Two 14" × 14" (36cm × 36cm) squares of orange, yellow, lime green and brown multicolor print

14" × 27½" (36cm × 70cm) piece of orange, yellow and lime green stripe print

Sixteen 5" × 5" (13cm × 13cm) squares of assorted yellow, orange, brown, tan and lime green prints

Note: I use the same combination of eight prints for the two patchwork blocks.

Scraps of tan stripe print (elephants' ears)

½ yard (½m) of brown print (border)

½ yard (½m) of lime green print (binding)

1⅝ yards (1½m) of any color print (backing and hanging sleeve)

CHENILLE

Two 9" × 9" (23cm × 23cm) squares and two 5" × 5" (13cm × 13cm) squares of white chenille

Note: You can substitute another fabric if chenille is not available.

WOOL FELT

Two 12" × 12" (30cm × 30cm) pieces of orange felt (elephants)

Scraps of orange felt (polka dots and flower centers), lime green felt (small flowers, leaves, polka dots and dots on elephants), brown felt (polka dots and elephants' feet), white felt (small flower and tail accents) and yellow felt (flower center)

supplies

1⅓ yards (1⅓m) quilt batting, 45" (114cm) wide

DMC cotton embroidery floss: white, #838 (brown), #471 (lime green), #744 (yellow) and #608 (orange)

Regular or lightweight paper-backed fusible web

¼" (6mm) orange button and two ¼" (6mm) yellow buttons

Materials and Tools (pages 8–10)

Pattern insert

Be sure to read the Techniques section and the individual project instructions thoroughly before you begin. Use two strands of embroidery floss for all stitching unless otherwise stated.

1 *Prepare the two polka dot blocks*

Cut two 14" × 14" (36cm × 36cm) squares of the multicolor print.

Cut two 9" × 9" (23cm × 23cm) squares of the white chenille.

Baste the chenille squares onto the center of the 14" × 14" (36cm × 36cm) squares. Blanket stitch around the chenille squares with four strands of the brown floss.

Referring to the pattern insert, trace and cut six polka dots: two from the orange felt, two from the brown felt and two from the green felt.

Referring to the project photo for placement, baste the polka dots onto the chenille squares, alternating the placement of the dots for each block.

Blanket stitch around the orange dots with the brown floss, around the brown dots with the white floss and around the green dots with the orange floss.

2 *Prepare the two patchwork blocks*

Cut sixteen 5" × 5" (13cm × 13cm) squares of the assorted prints.

Cut two 5" × 5" (13cm × 13cm) squares of white chenille.

Referring to the pattern insert, trace and cut two small flowers from the lime green felt and two small flower centers from the orange felt.

Baste the flower pieces onto the centers of the chenille squares.

Blanket stitch around the flowers with the brown floss. Straight stitch around the flower centers with the white floss.

Sew a ¼" (6mm) yellow button onto the center of each flower.

Lay the squares out for each block as desired, with the chenille flower square in the center. (Use the photo as a guide.) Sew the patchwork squares together.

3 *Prepare the elephant block*

Cut a 14" × 27½" (36cm × 70cm) piece of the orange, yellow and lime green stripe print.

Referring to the pattern insert, trace and cut two elephants from the orange felt, four feet from the brown felt, six dots and three leaves from the lime green felt, two tail accents and a small flower from the white felt and a small flower center from the yellow felt. Remember to cut one elephant in reverse so it will be facing the opposite direction.

Follow the Fusible Web Appliqué instructions on page 13 to fuse two elephant ears using the tan stripe print.

Referring to the photo and pattern for placement, baste the two elephant pieces facing each other, with the flower and leaves in the center, onto the stripe print fabric.

Blanket stitch around the elephants and tail accents with the brown floss, around the feet with the white floss and around the ears with the green floss. Add a single brown French knot to each elephant for the eyes. Add a yellow running stitch around the dots with a single white cross stitch in the center.

Blanket stitch around the flower with the orange floss. Straight stitch around the flower center with the green floss. Straight stitch around the leaves with the brown floss then add three running stitches along the center.

Sew a ¼" (6mm) orange button onto the flower center.

4 *Complete the quilt*

Refer to the General Instructions on page 16 to:

Piece the quilt top.

Add the border.

Assemble the layers.

Add a hanging sleeve.

Note: The hanging sleeve can be added after the binding if that is your preferred technique.

Add the binding.

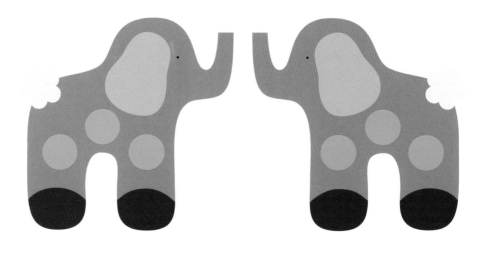

Baby Shower Idea

For a last-minute shower gift, whip up a "rub a dub dub" draw-string bath bag using leftover scraps of fabric. Fill the bag with an assortment of store-bought bath toys, baby shampoos, lotions, powders and a cute bath mitt. Mom can use the bath bag for added storage in the nursery. Adjust your fabric measurements as necessary to make larger gift bags for blankets or quilts. Or make miniature bags to fill with sweet treats for party favors.

mango tango polka dot pillow

fabric

COTTON PRINTS

Two 14" × 14" (36cm × 36cm) squares of orange, yellow, lime green and brown multicolor print

CHENILLE

9" × 9" (23cm × 23cm) square of white chenille

Note: You can substitute another fabric if chenille is not available.

WOOL FELT

Scraps of orange felt, lime green felt and brown felt (polka dots)

supplies

14" (36cm) square pillow form (or polyester fiberfill)

DMC cotton embroidery floss: white, #838 (brown) and #608 (orange)

Materials and Tools (pages 8–10)

Pattern insert

Be sure to read the Techniques section and the individual project instructions thoroughly before you begin. Use two strands of embroidery floss for all stitching unless otherwise stated.

1 Cut two 14" × 14" (36cm × 36cm) squares of the multicolor print.

2 Refer to the quilt instructions to make a polka dot block for the pillow front using a 14" × 14" (36cm × 36cm) fabric square. You will use the other square for the pillow backing.

3 Refer to the General Instructions on page 18 to finish the pillow.

mango tango patchwork pillow

fabric

COTTON PRINTS

Eight 5" × 5" (13cm × 13cm) squares of assorted yellow, orange, brown, tan and lime green prints

14" × 14" (36cm × 36cm) fabric square (backing)

CHENILLE

5" × 5" (13cm × 13cm) square of white chenille

Note: You can substitute another fabric if chenille is not available.

WOOL FELT

Scrap of lime green felt (small flower) and orange felt (flower center)

supplies

14" (36cm) square pillow form (or polyester fiberfill)

DMC cotton embroidery floss: white and #838 (brown)

¼" (6mm) yellow button

Materials and Tools (pages 8–10)

Pattern insert

Be sure to read the Techniques section and the individual project instructions thoroughly before you begin. Use two strands of embroidery floss for all stitching unless otherwise stated.

1 Cut a 14" × 14" (36cm × 36cm) square of the backing fabric.

2 Refer to the quilt instructions to make a patchwork flower block for the pillow front, using the eight fabric squares and the chenille square for the center.

3 Refer to the General Instructions on page 18 to finish the pillow.

mango tango pillow

fabric

COTTON PRINTS

Two 14" × 14" (36cm × 36cm) squares of orange, yellow and lime green plaid print

Scrap of tan stripe print (elephant's ear)

WOOL FELT

12" × 12" (30cm × 30cm) square of orange felt (elephant)

Scraps of lime green felt (leaves and dots on elephant; note that only two leaves are used for this project), brown (elephant's feet), white felt (small flower and tail accent) and yellow felt (flower center)

supplies

14" (36cm) square pillow form (or polyester fiberfill)

DMC cotton embroidery floss: white, #838 (brown), #471 (lime green), #744 (yellow) and #608 (orange)

Regular or lightweight paper-backed fusible web

¼" (6mm) orange button

Materials and Tools (pages 8–10)

Pattern insert

Be sure to read the Techniques section and the individual project instructions thoroughly before you begin. Use two strands of embroidery floss for all stitching unless otherwise stated.

1 Cut two 14" × 14" (36cm × 36cm) squares of the plaid print.

2 Refer to the quilt instructions to make an elephant block for the pillow front using a 14" × 14" (36cm × 36cm) fabric square. You will use the other square for the pillow backing.
Note: You can face the elephant motif in either direction, as shown on the center quilt block. Refer to this photo for placement of the flower and two leaves as well.

3 Refer to the General Instructions on page 18 to finish the pillow.

mango tango chenille wall hanging

fabric

COTTON PRINTS

Scrap of tan stripe print (elephant's ear)

CHENILLE

Two 24" × 24" (61cm × 61cm) squares of bright yellow chenille

14" × 14" (36cm × 36cm) square and four 5" × 5" (13cm × 13cm) squares of lime green chenille

WOOL FELT

12" × 12" (30cm × 30cm) square of orange felt (elephant)

Scraps of lime green felt (dots on elephant), brown felt (elephant's feet), white felt (small flowers and tail accent) and yellow felt (flower centers)

supplies

23" × 23" (58cm × 58cm) square of quilt batting

DMC cotton embroidery floss: white, #838 (brown), #471 (lime green), #744 (yellow) and #608 (orange)

Regular or lightweight paper-backed fusible web

Seven ¼" (6mm) orange buttons

2¾ yards (2½m) 1" (3cm) wide white pom-pom trim (optional)

Permanent fabric adhesive (such as Fabri-Tac) (optional)

Two 1" (3cm) plastic loops (for hanging)

Materials and Tools (8–10)

Pattern insert

Be sure to read the Techniques section and the individual project instructions thoroughly before you begin. Use two strands of embroidery floss for all stitching unless otherwise stated.

1 Cut two 24" × 24" (61cm × 61cm) squares of bright yellow chenille. Cut a 14" × 14" (36cm × 36cm) square and four 5" × 5" (13cm × 13cm) squares of the lime green chenille.

2 Cut a 23" × 23" (58cm × 58cm) square of the quilt batting.
Note: Due to the unfinished edges, the batting should be approximately 1" (3cm) less in total size compared to the chenille squares.

3 Referring to the pattern insert, trace and cut an elephant from the orange felt, two feet from the brown felt, three dots from the lime green felt, a tail accent and seven small flowers from the white felt and the seven circular flower centers from the yellow felt.

4 Follow the Fusible Web Appliqué instructions on page 13 to fuse the elephant's ear using the tan stripe print.

5 Baste the 14" × 14" (36cm × 36cm) green chenille square onto the center of a yellow chenille square. There should be 5" (13cm) on each side of the square.

6 Blanket stitch around the green chenille square with four strands of the brown floss.

7 Referring to the project photo and pattern for placement, baste the elephant pieces onto the center of the green chenille square.

8 Refer to the quilt instructions to embroider.

9 Referring to the project photo, baste three of the flowers, one onto the front foot and the other two overlapping the two edges of the green chenille square. Blanket stitch around the flowers with the orange floss. Straight stitch around the flower centers with the green floss. Sew the orange buttons onto the flower centers.

10 Baste the four 5" × 5" (13cm × 13cm) green chenille squares, one onto each corner. Baste the four remaining flowers onto the centers of the four squares. Embroider and add button trims as in Step 9.

11 Refer to the General Instructions on page 18 to complete the wall hanging. If desired, use permanent fabric adhesive to adhere the pom-pom trim to the back of the wall hanging.

POSH POODLE

oh la la! This Parisian-inspired collection, featuring pink poodles and feminine purses, can take tiny fashionistas all the way to their big-girl bedrooms in true style. Fluffy pink marabou trim imparts that extra touch of girly glamour.

posh poodle quilt

fabric

COTTON PRINTS

Two 14" × 14" (36cm × 36cm) squares of pink, white and black dot print

Twelve 5" × 5" (13cm × 13cm) squares of assorted pink and black prints

Note: I use the same combination of six prints for the two patchwork blocks.

9½" × 14" (24cm × 36cm) piece of black-and-white dot print

Scraps of black-and-white plaid (purse flap)

½ yard (½m) of white and pink print (border)

½ yard (½m) of black print for the binding

1⅝ yards (1½m) of any color print (backing and hanging sleeve)

CHENILLE

Two 14" × 14" (36cm × 36cm) squares of pink chenille

Note: You can substitute another fabric if chenille is not available.

WOOL FELT

Two 11" × 12" (28cm × 30cm) pieces of pink felt (poodle bodies)

Two 9" × 12" (23cm × 30cm) pieces of black felt (purses)

Scraps of pink felt (fluffy fur pieces, extra-large flower and miniature flower accents for the purses), black felt (purse handles and poodles' paws) and white felt (poodles' heads and legs and flower centers)

supplies

1⅓ yards (1¼m) quilt batting, 45" (114cm) wide

DMC cotton embroidery floss: white, #776 (pink) and #310 (black)

Regular or lightweight paper-backed fusible web

18" (46cm) pink marabou boa trim

Two ¼" (6mm) black buttons, two ⅜" (10mm) black buttons and a 1" (3cm) black button

20" (51cm) of ⅛" (3mm) wide black-and-white dot ribbon

Two ¾" (19mm) pink ribbon flowers

14" (36cm) of 1½" (4cm) wide black-and-white dot ribbon

Permanent fabric adhesive (such as Fabri-Tac)

Materials and Tools (pages 8–10)

Pattern insert

Be sure to read the Techniques section and the individual project instructions thoroughly before you begin. Use two strands of embroidery floss for all stitching unless otherwise stated.

1 *Prepare the two poodle blocks*

Cut two 14" × 14" (36cm × 36cm) squares of the pink, white and black dot print.

Referring to the pattern insert, trace and cut two poodle bodies and six fluffy fur pieces from the pink felt, two heads and four legs from the white felt and the four paws from the black felt.

Referring to the project photo and pattern insert for placement, baste the poodle pieces onto the center of the 14" × 14" (36cm × 36cm) squares.

Blanket stitch around the bodies and fluffy fur pieces with the black floss, around the head and legs with the pink floss and around the paws with the white floss. The eyes are two black French knots.

Sew a ⅜" (10mm) black button for each nose.

Cut two 10" (25cm) pieces of ⅛" (3mm) black-and-white dot ribbon and tie each piece into a bow. Stitch a bow and a pink ribbon flower onto the left side of each poodle head.

2 *Prepare the two purse blocks*

Cut two 14" × 14" (36cm × 36cm) squares of the pink chenille.

Referring to the pattern insert, trace and cut two 6" × 9" (15cm × 23cm) rectangular purse pieces and two handles from the black felt, two miniature flower accents from the pink felt and two miniature flower centers from the white felt.

Follow the Fusible Web Appliqué instructions on page 13 to fuse two purse flaps using the black-and-white plaid print.

Referring to the photo and pattern for placement, baste the purse pieces onto the centers of the pink chenille squares.

Blanket stitch around the purses and handles with the white floss, around the flaps with the pink floss and around the flower accents with the black floss. Add a pink running stitch around the circular flower centers.

Sew a ¼" (6mm) black button onto each flower center.

Cut the pink marabou trim into two 9" (23cm) pieces. Use permanent fabric adhesive to adhere the trim onto the top edges of the purses.

3 *Prepare the ribbon flower block*

Cut a 9½" × 14" (24cm × 36cm) piece of black-and-white dot print.

Referring to the pattern insert, trace and cut an extra-large flower from the pink felt and an extra-large flower center from the white felt.

Cut a 14" (36cm) piece of the 1½" (4cm) wide black-and-white dot ribbon. Baste the ribbon vertically along the center. Blanket stitch around the edges of the ribbon trim with the pink floss (or machine stitch if desired).

Referring to the project photo for placement, baste the flower pieces onto the center of the ribbon trim.

Blanket stitch around the flower with the black floss. Add a pink running stitch around the circular flower center.

Stitch a 1" (3cm) black button onto the flower center.

4 *Prepare the two patchwork blocks*

Cut twelve 5" × 5" (13cm × 13cm) squares of the assorted prints.

Lay out the squares for each block as desired to make three rows of two. (Use the project photo as a guide.) Sew the patchwork squares together.

5 *Complete the Quilt*

Refer to the General Instructions on page 16 to:

Piece the quilt top.

Add the border.

Assemble the layers.

Add a hanging sleeve.
Note: The hanging sleeve can be added after the binding if that is your preferred technique.

Add the binding.

Baby Shower Idea

Use the Posh Poodle collection as inspiration for a modern and trendy "Paris in Spring" baby shower theme. Decorate in pink, white and black accented with lots of fluffy marabou trim. Use invitations with purse or poodle motifs (or any Paris-themed attraction such as the Eiffel Tower). As refreshments, serve French-inspired appetizers or sweets along with sparkling pink champagne.

posh poodle purse pillow

fabric

COTTON PRINTS

Scrap of black-and-white plaid print (purse flap)

CHENILLE

Two 14" × 14" (36cm × 36cm) squares of pink chenille

Note: You can substitute another fabric if chenille is not available.

WOOL FELT

9" × 12" (23cm × 30cm) piece of black felt (purse)

Scraps of pink felt (miniature flower accent), black felt (handle) and white felt (flower center)

supplies

14" (36cm) square pillow form (or polyester fiberfill)

DMC cotton embroidery floss: white, #776 (pink) and #310 (black)

¼" (6mm) black button

Regular or lightweight paper-backed fusible web

9" (23cm) pink marabou boa trim

Permanent fabric adhesive (such as Fabri-Tac)

Materials and Tools (pages 8–10)

Pattern insert

Be sure to read the Techniques section and the individual project instructions thoroughly before you begin. Use two strands of embroidery floss for all stitching unless otherwise stated.

1 Cut two 14" × 14" (36cm × 36cm) squares of the pink chenille.

2 Refer to the quilt instructions to make a purse block for the pillow front using a 14" × 14" (36cm × 36cm) chenille square. You will use the other square for the pillow backing.

3 Refer to the General Instructions on page 18 to finish the pillow.

posh poodle pillow

fabric

COTTON PRINTS

Two 14" × 14" (36cm × 36cm) squares
of pink, white and black dot print

WOOL FELT

11" × 12" (28cm × 30cm) piece
of pink felt (body)

Scraps of pink felt (fluffy fur pieces), white
felt (head and legs) and black felt (paws)

supplies

14" (36cm) square pillow form
(or polyester fiberfill)

DMC cotton embroidery floss: white,
#776 (pink) and #310 (black)

⅜" (10mm) black button

10" (25cm) of ⅛" (3mm) wide
black-and-white dot ribbon

¾" (19mm) pink ribbon flower

1¾ yards (1¾m) of 1" (3cm) wide
white pom-pom trim (optional)

Permanent fabric adhesive (such
as Fabri-Tac) (optional)

Materials and Tools (pages 8–10)

Pattern insert

*Be sure to read the Techniques section
and the individual project instructions
thoroughly before you begin. Use two
strands of embroidery floss for all stitching
unless otherwise stated.*

1 Cut two 14" × 14" (36cm × 36cm)
squares of the dot print.

2 Refer to the quilt instructions
to make one of the poodle blocks
for the pillow front using a 14" × 14"
(36cm × 36cm) fabric square. You will use
the other square for the pillow backing.

3 Refer to the General Instructions on
page 18 to finish the pillow. If desired, use
permanent fabric adhesive to adhere
the pom-pom trim around the edges of
the pillow.

posh poodle flower pillow

fabric

COTTON PRINTS

Two 14" × 14" (36cm × 36cm) squares
of black-and-white dot print

WOOL FELT

Scraps of pink felt (extra-large flower)
and white felt (flower center)

supplies

14" (36cm) square pillow form
(or polyester fiberfill)

DMC cotton embroidery floss:
#776 (pink) and #310 (black)

1" (3cm) black button

28" (71cm) of 1½" (4cm) wide
black-and-white dot ribbon

Materials and Tools (pages 8–10)

Pattern insert

*Be sure to read the Techniques section
and the individual project instructions
thoroughly before you begin. Use two
strands of embroidery floss for all stitching
unless otherwise stated.*

1 Cut two 14" × 14" (36cm × 36cm)
squares of the dot print.

2 Cut two 14" (36cm) pieces of the 1½"
(4cm) wide dot ribbon. For the pillow
front, baste the two pieces of ribbon
onto one of the fabric squares so that
they intersect, approximately 5" (13cm)
from the top (horizontal piece) and 5"
(13cm) from the left side (vertical piece).
Refer to the quilt instructions to stitch
the ribbon and apply the flower motif so
that it overlaps the two ribbon pieces in
the center. You will use the other square
for the pillow backing.

3 Refer to the General Instructions on
page 18 to finish the pillow.

posh poodle chenille wall hanging

fabric

CHENILLE

Two 24" × 24" (61cm × 61cm) squares of pink chenille

14" × 14" (36cm × 36cm) square and four 5" × 5" (13cm × 13cm) squares of white chenille

WOOL FELT

11" × 12" (28cm × 30cm) piece of pink felt (body)

Scraps of pink felt (fluffy fur pieces and dots), white felt (head, legs and dots) and black felt (paws and dots)

supplies:

23" × 23" (58cm × 58cm) square of quilt batting

DMC cotton embroidery floss: white, #776 (pink) and #310 (black)

⅜" (10mm) black button

10" (25cm) of ⅛" (3mm) wide black-and-white dot ribbon

¾" (19mm) pink ribbon flower

2¾ yards (2½m) of 1" (3cm) wide white pom-pom trim (optional)

Permanent fabric adhesive (such as Fabri-Tac) (optional)

Two 1" (3cm) plastic loops (for hanging)

Materials and Tools (pages 8–10)

Pattern insert

Be sure to read the Techniques section and the individual project instructions thoroughly before you begin. Use two strands of embroidery floss for all stitching unless otherwise stated.

1 Cut two 24" × 24" (61cm × 61cm) squares of pink chenille. Cut a 14" × 14" (36cm × 36cm) square and four 5" × 5" (13cm × 13cm) squares of the white chenille.

2 Cut a 23" × 23" (58cm × 58cm) square of the quilt batting.
Note: Due to the unfinished edges, the batting should be approximately 1" (3cm) less in total size compared to the chenille squares.

3 Referring to the pattern insert, trace and cut a poodle body, three fluffy fur pieces and four dots from the pink felt, a poodle head, two legs and four dots from the white felt and two paws and four dots from the black felt.

4 Baste the 14" × 14" (36cm × 36cm) white chenille square onto the center of a pink chenille square. There should be 5" (13cm) on each side of the square.

5 Blanket stitch around the white chenille square with four strands of the black floss.

6 Referring to the project photo and pattern insert for placement, baste the poodle pieces onto the center of the white chenille square.

7 Refer to the quilt instructions to embroider and to add a button nose, bow and pink ribbon flower.

8 Baste the four 5" × 5" (13cm × 13cm) white chenille squares, one onto each corner. Baste the pink, white and black dots, one of each onto each of the four squares. Blanket stitch around the pink dots with the black floss, around the white dots with the pink floss and around the black dots with the white floss.

9 Refer to the General Instructions on page 18 to complete the wall hanging. If desired, add a decorative running stitch around the four corners using four strands of black floss. If desired, use permanent fabric adhesive to adhere the pom-pom trim around the back of the wall hanging.

BAYOU BUDDIES

Look what we found lurking in the swamp! This goofy gator and his froggie friends will inspire hours of adventure and imaginary fun on the bayou. With the playful mix of whimsy and style, this bright and bold collection is sure to please both moms and kids alike.

bayou buddies quilt

fabric

COTTON PRINTS

Two 14" × 14" (36cm × 36cm) squares of blue, yellow, lime green and white multi-stripe print

12½" × 27½" (32cm × 70cm) piece of blue gingham

Sixteen 5" × 5" (13cm × 13cm) squares of assorted blue, yellow and lime green prints **Note:** I use the same combination of eight prints for the two patchwork blocks.

½ yard (½m) of dark blue print (border)

½ yard (½m) of lime green print (binding)

1⅝ yards (1½m) of any color print (backing and hanging sleeve)

CHENILLE

Two 10" × 10" (25cm × 25cm) squares and two 5" × 5" (13cm × 13cm) squares of white chenille

Note: You can substitute another fabric if chenille is not available.

WOOL FELT

Two 10" × 11" (25cm × 28cm) pieces (frogs) and a 14" × 22" (36cm × 56cm) piece (alligator) of lime green felt (or fleece)

Two 7" × 13" (18cm × 33cm) pieces of blue felt (ponds)

Scraps of blue felt (dragonfly wings and alligator spots), yellow felt (alligator scales, dragonfly bodies and flower centers), white felt (small flowers, eyes and alligator's teeth), black felt (pupils) and red felt (frogs' tongues)

supplies

1⅓ yards (1¼m) quilt batting, 45" (114cm) wide

DMC cotton embroidery floss: white, #310 (black), #907 (lime green), #157 (blue) and 744 (yellow)

25" (64cm) jumbo white rickrack

Materials and Tools (pages 8–10)

Pattern insert

Be sure to read the Techniques section and the individual project instructions thoroughly before you begin. Use two strands of embroidery floss for all stitching unless otherwise stated.

1 *Prepare the two frog blocks*

Cut two 14"× 14" (36cm × 36cm) squares of the multi-stripe print.

Cut two 10" × 10" (25cm × 25cm) squares of the white chenille.

Referring to the pattern insert, trace and cut two frogs from the lime green felt (or fleece), two ponds from the blue felt, four eyes and two small flowers from the white felt, four pupils from the black felt, two tongues from the red felt and two circular flower centers from the yellow felt.

Baste the chenille squares onto the centers of the 14"× 14" (36cm × 36cm) squares.

Referring to the project photo and pattern insert for placement, baste the frog pieces, ponds and flowers onto the white chenille squares. (Remember to alternate the position of the pupils so that the top frog is looking down and the bottom frog is looking up. Alternate the position of the flowers as well.) Set the tongue pieces aside until after the mouths are stitched.

Blanket stitch around the chenille squares using four strands of the green floss.

Blanket stitch around the frogs and flowers with the black floss and around the ponds with the yellow floss. Straight stitch around the flower centers with the blue floss. Add a black running stitch around the eyes and pupils. Satin stitch the nostrils with black floss. Trace, then backstitch the mouths with black floss. Add a black French knot at the ends of each mouth.

Baste the two tongues underneath the mouths (alternating the position). Add a white running stitch around each tongue.

2 *Prepare the two patchwork blocks*

Cut sixteen 5" × 5" (13cm × 13cm) squares of the assorted prints.

Cut two 5" × 5" (13cm × 13cm) squares of white chenille.

Referring to the pattern insert, trace and cut two dragonfly bodies from the yellow felt and two wings from the blue felt.

Baste the dragonfly pieces at a slight angle onto the center of the chenille squares (facing center).

Blanket stitch around the wings with the black floss. Add a running stitch around the bodies and two tiny cross stitches for the eyes using a single strand of black floss. The noses are white French knots. Trace, then backstitch the antennas with four strands of the green floss.

Lay out the squares for each block as desired, with the chenille dragonfly square in the center. (Use the photo as a guide.) Sew the patchwork squares together.

3 _Prepare the alligator block_

Cut a 12½" × 27½" (32cm × 70cm) piece of the blue gingham.

Cut two 12½" (32cm) pieces of jumbo white rickrack. Baste, then stitch the two pieces vertically, approximately 2½" (6cm) from each side.

Referring to the pattern insert, trace and cut an alligator from the lime green felt (or fleece), five spots from the blue felt, three scales from the yellow felt, two eyes and three teeth from the white felt and two pupils from the black felt.

Referring to the photo and pattern insert for placement, baste the alligator pieces onto the center of the blue gingham fabric in between the rickrack trim. Set the three teeth aside until after the mouth is stitched.

Blanket stitch around the alligator with the black floss and around the spots with the white floss. Add a green running stitch around the scales. Add a black running stitch around the eyes and pupils. Trace, then backstitch the mouth with the black floss. Add a black French knot at the end of the mouth.

Baste the three teeth spaced evenly underneath the mouth. Add a black running stitch around each tooth.

4 _Complete the quilt_

Refer to the General Instructions on page 16 to:

Piece the quilt top.

Add the border.

Assemble the layers.

Add a hanging sleeve.
Note: The hanging sleeve can be added after the binding if that is your preferred technique.

Add the binding.

Decorating Tips

Throw rugs are both functional and decorative and allow you to change the look of the room without the added expense of altering the flooring. To make a big splash in the kids' bathroom, purchase an inexpensive bath mat and embroider a fun felt frog inspired by the Bayou Buddies collection.

bayou buddies alligator pillow

fabric

COTTON PRINTS

Two 14" × 23" (36cm × 58cm)
pieces of blue gingham

WOOL FELT

14" × 22" (36cm × 56cm) piece of lime
green felt (or fleece) (alligator)

Scraps of blue felt (spots), yellow felt (scales),
white felt (eyes and teeth) and black felt (pupils)

supplies

Polyester fiberfill

DMC cotton embroidery floss: white,
#310 (black) and #907 (lime green)

28" (71cm) jumbo white rickrack

Materials and Tools (pages 8–10)

Pattern insert

*Be sure to read the Techniques section
and the individual project instructions
thoroughly before you begin. Use two
strands of embroidery floss for all stitching
unless otherwise stated.*

1 Cut two 14" × 23" (36cm × 58cm)
pieces of the blue gingham.

2 Cut two 14" (36cm) pieces of jumbo
white rickrack. Baste, then stitch the two
pieces vertically onto the front of one
of the pillow pieces, approximately 2½"
(6cm) from each side.

3 Refer to the quilt instructions to
make an alligator block for the pillow
front using the 14" × 23" (36cm × 58cm)
piece of blue gingham with the rickrack
trim. You will use the other piece for the
pillow backing. (Note that the alligator
will be overlapping the rickrack trim.)

4 Refer to the quilt instructions to
embroider.

5 Refer to the General Instructions on
page 18 to finish the pillow, using fiberfill
to stuff rather than a pillow form.

bayou buddies pillow

fabric

COTTON PRINTS

Two 14" × 14" (36cm × 36cm) squares of blue, yellow, lime green and white multi-stripe print

CHENILLE

10" × 10" (25cm × 25cm) square of white chenille

Note: You can can substitute another fabric if chenille is not available.

WOOL FELT

10" × 11" (25cm × 28cm) piece of lime green felt (or fleece) (frog)

7" × 13" (18cm × 33cm) piece of blue felt (pond)

Scraps of yellow felt (flower center), white felt (eyes and small flower), black felt (pupils) and red felt (tongue)

supplies

14" (36cm) square pillow form (or polyester fiberfill)

DMC cotton embroidery floss: white, #310 (black), #907 (lime green), #157 (blue) and #744 (yellow)

Materials and Tools (pages 8–10)

Pattern insert

Be sure to read the Techniques section and the individual project instructions thoroughly before you begin. Use two strands of embroidery floss for all stitching unless otherwise stated.

1 Cut two 14" × 14" (36cm × 36cm) squares of the multi-stripe print.

2 Refer to the quilt instructions to make a frog block for the pillow front using a 14" × 14" (36cm × 36cm) fabric square. You will use the other square for the pillow backing.

3 Refer to the General Instructions on page 18 to finish the pillow.

bayou buddies patchwork pillow

fabric

COTTON PRINTS

Eight 5" × 5" (13cm × 13cm) squares of
assorted blue, yellow and lime green prints

14" × 14" (36cm × 36cm) square
of any color fabric (backing)

CHENILLE

5" × 5" (13cm × 13cm) square of white chenille

Note: You can substitute another
fabric if chenille is not available.

WOOL FELT

Scraps of blue felt (dragonfly wings)
and yellow felt (dragonfly body)

supplies

14" (36cm) square pillow form
(or polyester fiberfill)

DMC cotton embroidery floss: white,
#310 (black) and #907 (lime green)

Materials and Tools (pages 8–10)

Pattern insert

*Be sure to read the Techniques section
and the individual project instructions
thoroughly before you begin. Use two
strands of embroidery floss for all
stitching unless otherwise stated.*

1 Cut a 14" × 14" (36cm × 36cm) square
of the backing fabric.

2 Refer to the quilt instructions to
make a patchwork dragonfly block for
the pillow front, using the eight fabric
squares and the chenille square for
the center.

3 Refer to the General Instructions on
page 18 to finish the pillow.

bayou buddies chenille wall hanging

fabric

CHENILLE

Two 22" × 22" (56cm × 56cm) squares of white chenille

12" × 12" (30cm × 30cm) square of blue chenille

Four 5" × 5" (13cm × 13cm) squares of lime green chenille

WOOL FELT

12" × 12" (30cm × 30cm) square of lime green felt (or fleece) (frog)

Scraps of white felt (eyes and small flowers), black felt (pupils), red felt (tongue) and yellow felt (flower centers)

supplies

21" × 21" (53cm × 53cm) square of quilt batting

DMC cotton embroidery floss: white, #310 (black) and #157 (blue)

Two 1" (3cm) plastic loops (for hanging)

Materials and Tools (pages 8–10)

Pattern insert

Be sure to read the Techniques section and the individual project instructions thoroughly before you begin. Use two strands of embroidery floss for all stitching unless otherwise stated.

1 Cut two 22" × 22" (56cm × 56cm) squares of white chenille. Cut a 12" × 12" (30cm × 30cm) square of blue chenille and four 5" × 5" (13cm × 13cm) squares of lime green chenille.

2 Cut a 21" × 21" (53cm × 53cm) square of the quilt batting.
Note: Due to the unfinished edges, the batting should be approximately 1" (3cm) less in total size compared to the chenille squares.

3 Referring to the pattern insert, trace and cut the frog from the lime green felt, two eyes and five small flowers from the white felt, two pupils from the black felt, a tongue from the red felt and five small flower centers from the yellow felt.

4 Baste the blue chenille square onto the center of one of the white chenille squares. There should be 5" (13cm) on each side of the square.

5 Blanket stitch around the blue chenille square with four strands of the black floss.

6 Referring to the project photo and pattern insert for placement, baste the frog and flower pieces onto the center of the blue chenille square. Set the tongue piece aside until after the mouth is stitched.

7 Refer to the quilt instructions to embroider.

8 Baste the four 5" × 5" (13cm × 13cm) lime green chenille squares, one onto each corner. Baste the four remaining flowers onto the centers of the four squares. Embroider the flowers as in the quilt instructions.

9 Refer to the General Instructions on page 18 to complete the wall hanging.

Baby Shower Idea

Stitch a keepsake gift tag using leftover scraps of wool felt. Simply cut two pieces of felt into a gift tag shape. Decorate the front piece by stitching the baby's name, then add decorative trims such as buttons, rosebuds or rickrack. Stitch the two tag pieces together, punch a hole at the top and tie with ribbon trim. Mom can use the tag to decorate the nursery or add it to her baby shower scrapbook.

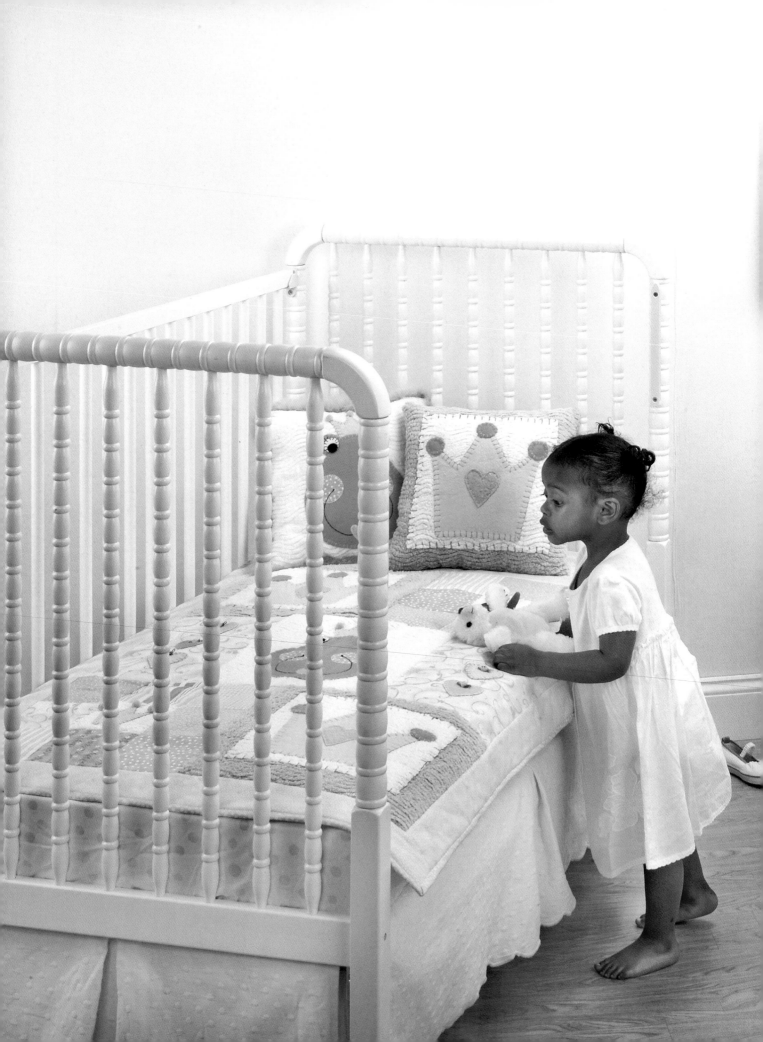

PRINCESS LILY

Little princesses will love dreaming in this magical storybook kingdom. Complete with fairy-tale frogs, jeweled crowns and heavenly hearts, this enchanting collection of dream décor will inspire hours of fantasy play and happily-ever-afters.

princess lily quilt

fabric

COTTON PRINTS

Two 8¼" × 14" (21cm × 36cm) pieces of a multicolor pastel print in pink, yellow and green

Tip: Look for fairy-tale or princess-themed prints. I chose one with flowers and delicate scrolls.

Sixteen 5" × 5" (13cm × 13cm) squares of assorted pink, yellow, lavender and green prints

Note: I use the same combination of eight prints for the two patchwork blocks.

Scraps of pink dot print (cheeks)

½ yard (½m) of yellow print (border)

½ yard (½m) of lavender print (binding)

1⅝ yards (1½m) of any color print (backing and hanging sleeve)

CHENILLE

Two 14" × 14" (36cm × 36cm) squares of lavender chenille

Two 10" × 10" (25cm × 25cm) squares, two 5" × 5" (13cm × 13cm) squares and a 12" × 14" (30cm × 36cm) piece of white chenille

Note: You can substitute another fabric if chenille is not available.

WOOL FELT

11" × 12" (28cm × 30cm) piece of lime green felt (frog)

Two 11" × 11" (28cm × 28cm) squares of yellow felt (large crowns)

Scraps of lime green felt (hearts and jewel dots on the crowns), yellow felt (hearts and smaller crowns), pink felt (hearts and lips), white felt (eyes) and black felt (pupils)

supplies

1⅓ yards (1¼m) quilt batting, 45" (114cm) wide

DMC cotton embroidery floss: white, #310 (black), #727(yellow), #209 (lavender) and #907 (lime green)

Regular or lightweight paper-backed fusible web

Nine ½" (13mm) pink pom-poms

Six ¾" (19mm) ribbon rosebuds: two pink, two yellow and two lavender

Materials and Tools (pages 8–10)

Pattern insert

Be sure to read the Techniques section and the individual project instructions thoroughly before you begin. Use two strands of embroidery floss for all stitching unless otherwise stated.

1 *Prepare the two crown blocks*

Cut two 14" × 14" (36cm × 36cm) squares of the lavender chenille.

Cut two 10" × 10" (25cm × 25cm) squares of the white chenille.

Referring to the pattern insert, trace and cut two large crowns from the yellow felt, six round jewels from the lime green felt and two hearts from the pink felt.

Baste the white chenille squares onto the centers of the lavender chenille squares. Blanket stitch around the white chenille square using four strands of the green floss.

Referring to the project photo and pattern insert for placement, baste the crown pieces onto the centers of the white chenille squares.

Blanket stitch around the crowns with the lavender floss and around the jewels with the yellow floss. Add a white running stitch around the hearts.

2 *Prepare the two patchwork blocks*

Cut sixteen 5" × 5" (13cm × 13cm) squares of the assorted prints.

Cut two 5" × 5" (13cm × 13cm) squares of white chenille.

Referring to the pattern insert, trace and cut two small crowns from the yellow felt.

Baste the crowns onto the center of the chenille squares.

Blanket stitch around each crown with the lavender floss.

Lay out the squares for each block as desired, with the chenille crown square in the center. (Use the photo as a guide.) Sew the patchwork squares together.

Stitch three pink pom-poms onto the pointed tips of each crown.

3 *Prepare the frog block*

Cut a 12" × 14" (30cm × 36cm) piece of the white chenille.

Referring to the pattern insert, trace and cut a frog from the lime green felt, a small crown from the yellow felt, a lips piece from the pink felt, two eyes from the white felt and two pupils from the black felt.

Follow the Fusible Web Appliqué instructions on page 13 to fuse the cheeks onto the frog using the pink dot print.

Referring to the photo and pattern for placement, baste the crown and frog pieces onto the center of the chenille background.

Blanket stitch around the frog with the yellow floss, around the crown with the lavender floss, around the cheeks and lips with the white floss and around the eyes with the black floss. Use a black running stitch to secure the pupils. Add three black straight stitches for the eyelashes. Trace, then backstitch the mouth with the black floss, beginning at each side of the lips. Add a black French knot at each end of the mouth.

Stitch three pink pom-poms onto the pointed tips of the crown.

4 *Prepare the two heart blocks*

Cut two 8¼" × 14" (21cm × 36cm) pieces of the multicolor pastel print.

Referring to the pattern insert, trace and cut six hearts, two from the pink felt, two from the yellow felt and two from the lime green felt.

Referring to the project photo for placement, baste a pink, green and yellow heart onto each of the fabric pieces. Vary the order of the colors as desired.

Blanket stitch around the pink hearts with the white floss, around the green hearts with the yellow floss and around the yellow hearts with the lavender floss.

Stitch the ribbon rosebuds onto the top center of the hearts: yellow rosebuds on the pink hearts, pink rosebuds on the green hearts and lavender rosebuds on the yellow hearts.

5 *Complete the quilt*

Refer to the General Instructions on page 16 to:

Piece the quilt top.

Add the border.

Assemble the layers.

Add a hanging sleeve.
Note: The hanging sleeve can be added after the binding if that is your preferred technique.

Add the binding.

Baby Shower Idea

Welcome her royal majesty with a Pink Princess baby shower inspired by the Princess Lily collection. Decorate with pink tulle and princess-themed decorations such as crowns, fairy-tale frogs and storybook castles. Have princess party hats or tiaras for guests to wear, along with wands as party favors. For a great centerpiece, top the shower cake with a dollar-store tiara or serve princess cupcakes frosted with pink icing and colorful candy sprinkles and displayed on a tiered stand.

princess lily patchwork pillow

fabric

COTTON PRINTS

Eight 5" × 5" (13cm × 13cm) squares of assorted pink, yellow, lavender and green prints

14" × 14" (36cm × 36cm) square of any color fabric (backing)

CHENILLE

5" × 5" (13cm × 13cm) square of white chenille

Note: You can substitute another fabric if chenille is not available.

WOOL FELT

Scrap of yellow felt (small crown)

supplies

14" (36cm) square pillow form (or polyester fiberfill)

DMC cotton embroidery floss: #209 (lavender)

Three ½" (13mm) pink pom-poms

Materials and Tools (pages 8–10)

Pattern insert

Be sure to read the Techniques section and the individual project instructions thoroughly before you begin. Use two strands of embroidery floss for all stitching unless otherwise stated.

1 Cut a 14" × 14" (36cm × 36cm) square of the backing fabric.

2 Refer to the quilt instructions to make a patchwork crown block for the pillow front, using the eight fabric squares and the chenille square for the center.

3 Refer to the General Instructions on page 18 to finish the pillow.

princess lily crown pillow

fabric

CHENILLE

Two 14" × 14" (36cm × 36cm) squares of lavender chenille

10" × 10" (25cm × 25cm) square of white chenille

Note: You can substitute another fabric if chenille is not available.

WOOL FELT

11" × 11" (28cm × 28cm) square of yellow felt (large crown)

Scraps of lime green felt (jewel dots on crown) and pink felt (heart)

supplies

14" (36cm) square pillow form (or polyester fiberfill)

DMC cotton embroidery floss: white, #727 (yellow), #209 (lavender) and #907 (lime green)

Materials and Tools (pages 8–10)

Pattern insert

Be sure to read the Techniques section and the individual project instructions thoroughly before you begin. Use two strands of embroidery floss for all stitching unless otherwise stated.

1 Cut two 14" × 14" (36cm × 36cm) squares of the lavender chenille.

2 Refer to the quilt instructions to make a crown block for the pillow front using one of the 14" × 14" (36cm × 36cm) chenille squares. You will use the other square for the pillow backing.

3 Refer to the General Instructions on page 18 to finish the pillow.

princess lily pillow

fabric

COTTON PRINTS

Scraps of pink dot print (cheeks)

CHENILLE

Two 14" × 14" (36cm × 36cm) squares of white chenille

Note: You can substitute another fabric if chenille is not available.

WOOL FELT

11" × 12" (28cm × 30cm) piece of lime green felt (frog)

Scraps of yellow felt (small crown), white felt (eyes), black felt (pupils) and pink felt (lips)

supplies

14" (36cm) square pillow form (or polyester fiberfill)

DMC cotton embroidery floss: white, #310 (black), #727 (yellow) and #209 (lavender)

Regular or lightweight paper-backed fusible web

Three ½" (13mm) pink pom poms

1¾ yards (1¾m) lavender marabou boa trim

Permanent fabric adhesive (such as Fabri-Tac)

Materials and Tools (pages 8–10)

Pattern insert

Be sure to read the Techniques section and the individual project instructions thoroughly before you begin. Use two strands of embroidery floss for all stitching unless otherwise stated.

1 Cut two 14" × 14" (36cm × 36cm) squares of the white chenille.

2 Refer to the quilt instructions to make a frog block for the pillow front using a 14" × 14" (36cm × 36cm) chenille square. You'll use the other square for the pillow backing.

3 Refer to the General Instructions on page 18 to finish the pillow. Use permanent fabric adhesive to adhere the marabou trim around the edges of the pillow.

princess lily chenille wall hanging

fabric

COTTON PRINTS

Scraps of pink dot print (cheeks)

CHENILLE

Two 24" × 24" (61cm × 61cm)
squares of lavender chenille

14" × 14" (36cm × 36cm) square and four 5" × 5"
(13cm × 13cm) squares of white chenille

WOOL FELT

11" × 12" (28cm × 30cm) piece
of lime green felt (frog)

Scraps of yellow felt (small crown),
pink felt (hearts and lips), white felt
(eyes) and black felt (pupils)

supplies

23" × 23" (58cm × 58cm) square of quilt batting

DMC cotton embroidery floss: white,
#310 (black), #727 (yellow), #209
(lavender) and #907 (lime green)

Regular or lightweight paper-backed fusible web

Three ½" (13mm) pink pom-poms

Four ¾" (19mm) yellow ribbon rosebuds

Two 1" (3cm) plastic loops (for hanging)

Materials and Tools (pages 8–10)

Pattern insert

*Be sure to read the Techniques section
and the individual project instructions
thoroughly before you begin. Use two
strands of embroidery floss for all stitching
unless otherwise stated.*

1 Cut two 24" × 24" (61cm × 61cm)
squares of lavender chenille. Cut a
14" × 14" (36cm × 36cm) square and four
5" × 5" (13cm × 13cm) squares of the
white chenille.

2 Cut a 23" × 23" (58cm × 58cm)
square of the quilt batting.
Note: Due to the unfinished edges,
the batting should be approximately 1"
(3cm) less in total size compared to the
chenille squares.

3 Referring to the pattern insert, trace
and cut a frog from the lime green felt,
a small crown from the yellow felt, four
hearts and a lips piece from the pink felt,
two eyes from the white felt and two
pupils from the black felt.

4 Follow the Fusible Web Appliqué
instructions on page 13 to fuse two
cheeks onto the frog using the pink
dot print.

5 Baste the 14" × 14" (36cm × 36cm)
white chenille square onto the center
of one of the lavender chenille squares.
There should be 5" (13cm) on each side of
the square.

6 Blanket stitch around the white
chenille square with four strands of the
pink floss.

7 Referring to the project photo and
pattern insert for placement, baste the
crown and frog pieces onto the center of
the white chenille square.

8 Refer to the quilt instructions to
embroider and add pom-pom trims to
the crown.

9 Baste the four 5" × 5" (13cm × 13cm)
white chenille squares, one onto each
corner. Baste the four hearts onto the
centers of the four squares. Blanket stitch
around the hearts with the white floss.
Stitch a yellow ribbon rosebud onto the
top center of each heart.

10 Refer to the General Instructions
on page 18 to complete the wall hanging.
If desired, add a decorative running
stitch around the four corners using four
strands of the lime green floss.

BUTTERFLY GARDEN

Springtime butterflies and freshly picked blossoms create a sweet retreat for pint-size flutter bugs. Ribbons, rosebuds and button trims add their charm to this enchanting garden theme.

The quilts, pillows and blankets placed in cribs are for photographic purposes only. Never put your baby to bed with these soft bedding items as they may present a serious safety hazard.

butterfly garden quilt

fabric

COTTON PRINTS

Two 14" × 14" (36cm × 36cm) squares of pale green and pink floral print

Twelve 5" × 5" (13cm × 13cm) squares of assorted pink, green, lavender and yellow prints. **Note:** I use the same combination of six prints for the two blocks.

Scraps of lavender dot print (extra-large flowers), pale green dot print (leaves) and pink dot print (cheeks and flower centers)

½ yard (½m) of lavender print (border)

½ yard (½m) of pink print (binding)

1⅝ yards (1½m) of any color print (backing and hanging sleeve)

CHENILLE

Two 14" × 14" (36cm × 36cm) squares of bright pink chenille

9½" × 14" (24cm × 36cm) piece of cream chenille

Note: You can substitute another fabric if chenille is not available.

WOOL FELT

Two 13" × 13" (33cm × 33cm) squares of pink felt (butterfly wings)

Two 12" × 12" (30cm × 30cm) squares of yellow felt

Scraps of pink felt (extra-large flower), yellow felt (dots on wings and flower center), cream felt (butterfly bodies and flower centers) and pastel green felt (leaves, dots on wings and flower center)

supplies

1⅓ yards (1⅓m) quilt batting, 45" (114cm) wide

6" (15cm) jumbo pale green rickrack

DMC cotton embroidery floss: ecru, #3716 (pink), #368 (green), #209 (lavender) and #727 (yellow)

Regular or lightweight paper-backed fusible web

Nine ½" (13mm) lavender buttons, two ½" (13mm) yellow buttons, two ¼" (6mm) pink buttons and five ¼" (6mm) yellow buttons

10" (25cm) of ⅛" (3mm) wide pink dot ribbon

¾" (19mm) pink ribbon rosebud

Materials and Tools (pages 8–10)

Pattern insert

Be sure to read the Techniques section and the individual project instructions thoroughly before you begin. Use two strands of embroidery floss for all stitching unless otherwise stated.

1 *Prepare the two butterfly blocks*

Cut two 14" × 14" (36cm × 36cm) squares of the pale green and pink floral print.

Referring to the pattern insert, trace and cut two butterfly bodies from the cream felt, two wings from the pink felt, eight large dots from the yellow felt and eight small dots from the pastel green felt.

Follow the Fusible Web Appliqué instructions on page 13 to fuse two cheeks onto each felt butterfly using the pink dot print.

Referring to the project photo and pattern insert for placement, baste the butterfly pieces onto the 14" × 14" (36cm × 36cm) squares.

Blanket stitch around the butterfly bodies with the green floss, around the wings with the lavender floss and around the cheeks with the ecru floss. Straight stitch around the yellow dots with the ecru floss. Add a pink running stitch around the pale green dots with an ecru cross stitch in the center. Trace, then backstitch the antennas with the lavender floss. The eyes are two lavender French knots. Add three pink cross stitches spaced evenly along the body.

Sew a ¼" (3mm) pink button for each nose.

2 *Prepare the two square flower blocks*

Cut two 14" × 14" (36cm × 36cm) squares of the bright pink chenille.

Cut two 9" × 9" (23cm × 23cm) squares of the yellow felt and two extra-large flower centers from the cream felt.

Follow the Fusible Web Appliqué instructions to fuse three leaves onto each yellow felt square using the pale green dot print. Fuse an extra-large flower onto each yellow felt square using the lavendar dot print.

Baste the felt flower centers.

Fuse the smaller flower centers to the flowers using the pink dot print.

Baste the yellow felt squares onto the centers of the pink chenille squares.

Blanket stitch around the squares with the green floss, around the flowers with the pink floss, around the leaves with the lavender floss and around the pink flower centers with the ecru floss. Add a green running stitch around the cream felt flower centers.

Sew four ½" (13mm) lavender buttons onto the corners of each yellow felt square and a ½" (13mm) yellow button onto each pink flower center.

3 *Prepare the rectangular flower block*

Cut a 9½" × 14" (24cm × 36cm) piece of cream chenille.

Referring to the pattern insert, trace and cut an extra-large flower from the pink felt, an extra-large flower center from the yellow felt and two leaves and a smaller flower center from the pastel green felt.

Cut a 6" (15cm) piece of the jumbo pale green rickrack for the flower stem. Baste the rickrack piece from the bottom center onto the chenille block. Secure using a green running stitch (or machine stitch if desired).

Referring to the project photo for placement, baste the flower pieces and leaves onto the chenille block.

Blanket stitch around the flower with the green floss and around the pale green flower center with the pink floss. Straight stitch around the leaves with the lavender floss, then add three yellow running stitches along the center. Add a lavender running stitch around the yellow flower center. Add five decorative swirls, one onto each petal, using a running stitch and the ecru floss.

Sew a ½" (13mm) lavender button onto the flower center and a ¼" (6mm) yellow button onto the center of each decorative swirl.

Tie a bow with a 10" (25cm) piece of the pink dot ribbon. Stitch the bow and pink rosebud onto the top of the flower stem.

4 *Prepare the two patchwork blocks*

Cut twelve 5" × 5" (13cm × 13cm) squares of the assorted prints.

Lay out the squares for each block as desired to make three rows of two. (Use the project photo as a guide.) Sew the patchwork squares together.

5 *Complete the quilt*

Refer to the General Instructions on page 16 to:

Piece the quilt top.

Add the border.

Assemble the layers.

Add a hanging sleeve.
Note: The hanging sleeve can be added after the binding if that is your preferred technique.

Add the binding.

Baby Shower Idea

A romantic garden party gathering is a wonderful way to celebrate a spring or summer baby shower. Use the Butterfly Garden collection as inspiration, decorating with lots of pastel bugs and blossoms. Use terra-cotta garden pots to serve yummy desserts or fill miniature pots with sweet treats as take-home favors.

butterfly garden felt accent

fabric

||||||||||||||||||||||||||||||||

COTTON PRINTS

Scraps of pink dot print (cheeks)

WOOL FELT

Two 13" × 13" (33cm × 33cm) squares
of pink felt (butterfly wings)

Scraps of cream felt (butterfly body),
yellow felt (dots on wings) and pastel
green felt (dots on wings)

supplies

||||||||||||||||||||||||||||||||

Polyester fiberfill

DMC cotton embroidery floss: ecru, #3716
(pink), #368 (green) and #209 (lavender)

Regular or lightweight paper-backed fusible web

¼" (6mm) pink button

12" (30cm) of ⅜" (10mm) wide
pink dot ribbon (for hanger)

20" (51cm) of ⅛" (3mm) wide pink dot ribbon

Two ¾" (19mm) pink ribbon rosebuds

8" (20cm) of ⅛" (3mm) wide
lavender dot ribbon

Permanent fabric adhesive (such as Fabri-Tac)

Materials and Tools (pages 8–10)

Pattern insert

*Be sure to read the Techniques section
and the individual project instructions
thoroughly before you begin. Use two
strands of embroidery floss for all stitching
unless otherwise stated.*

1 Referring to the pattern insert, trace
and cut two butterfly bodies from the
cream felt, two wings from the pink felt,
four large dots from the yellow felt and
four small dots from the pastel green felt.

2 Follow the Fusible Web Appliqué
instructions on page 13 to fuse the cheek
circles using the pink dot print. Blanket
stitch around the cheeks with the
ecru floss.

3 Add two French knots for the eyes
with the lavender floss. Stitch a ¼" (6mm)
pink button for the nose. Add three
pink cross stitches spaced evenly along
the body.

4 Referring to the project photo and
pattern insert for placement, baste the
yellow and green dots onto one of the
wing pieces. Straight stitch around the
yellow dots with the ecru floss. Add
a pink running stitch around the pale
green dots with an ecru cross stitch in
the center.

5 Cut two 4" (10cm) pieces of the
lavender dot ribbon. Use permanent
fabric adhesive to glue the ends into
a loop shape. Use a tiny dab of the
adhesive to adhere the antennas to the
back of the front body piece.

6 Place the two body pieces wrong
sides together. Pin the two body piece
layers onto the center of the front
decorated wing piece. Set aside the back
wing piece, which will be stitched on later.

7 Blanket stitch around the body with
the green floss, stitching through the
wing piece where it overlaps. This will
secure the body onto the front of the
wings. Be sure to leave an opening large
enough for stuffing with fiberfill.

8 Stuff the body with fiberfill, then
blanket stitch the opening closed.

9 Place the two wing pieces wrong
sides together. Pin if desired. Blanket
stitch around the wings with the lavender
floss, leaving an opening large enough
for stuffing. Stuff the wings, then blanket
stitch the opening closed.

10 Cut a 12" (30cm) piece of the
⅜" (10mm) wide pink dot ribbon. Stitch
the ends of the ribbon onto the top of
the wings for a hanger. Stitch or glue
the rosebud trims onto the ends of
the hanger.

11 Cut two 10" (25cm) pieces of the
⅛" (3mm) wide pink dot ribbon and tie
each piece into a bow. Stitch or glue the
bows just above the rosebud trims.

butterfly garden flower pillow

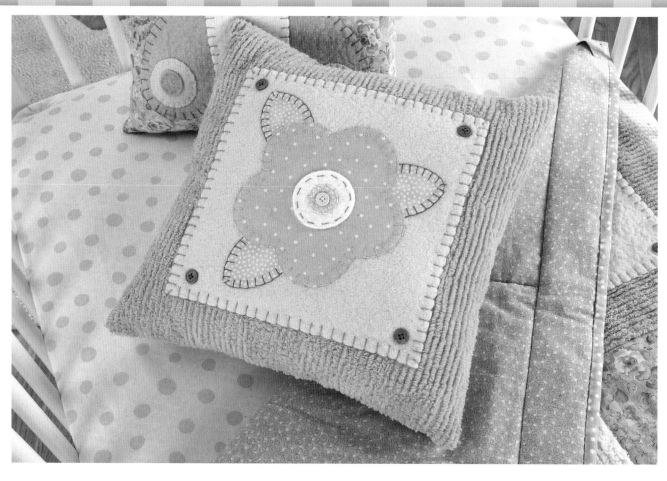

fabric

COTTON PRINTS

Scraps of lavender dot print (extra-large flower), pale green dot print (leaves) and pink dot print (flower center)

CHENILLE

Two 14" × 14" (36cm × 36cm) squares of bright pink chenille

Note: You can substitute another fabric if chenille is not available.

WOOL FELT

12" × 12" (30cm × 30cm) square of yellow felt

Scrap of cream felt (flower center)

supplies

14" (36cm) square pillow form (or polyester fiberfill)

DMC cotton embroidery floss: ecru, #3716 (pink), #368 (green) and #209 (lavender)

Regular or lightweight paper-backed fusible web

Buttons: four ½" (13mm) lavender and a ½" (13mm) yellow

Materials and Tools (pages 8–10)

Pattern insert

Be sure to read the Techniques section and the individual project instructions thoroughly before you begin. Use two strands of embroidery floss for all stitching unless otherwise stated.

1 Cut two 14" × 14" (36cm × 36cm) squares of the bright pink chenille.

2 Refer to the quilt instructions to make a flower block for the pillow front using a 14" × 14" (36cm × 36cm) chenille square. You will use the other square for the pillow backing.

3 Refer to the General Instructions on page 18 to finish the pillow.

butterfly garden pillow

fabric

COTTON PRINTS

Two 14" × 14" (36cm × 36cm) squares of pale green and pink floral print

Scraps of pink dot print (cheeks)

WOOL FELT

13" × 13" (33cm × 33cm) square of pink felt (butterfly wings)

Scraps of yellow felt (dots on wings), cream felt (butterfly body) and pastel green felt (dots on wings)

supplies

14" (36cm) square pillow form (or polyester fiberfill)

DMC cotton embroidery floss: ecru, #3716 (pink), #368 (green) and #209 (lavender)

Regular or lightweight paper-backed fusible web

¼" (6mm) pink button

Materials and Tools (pages 8–10)

Pattern insert

Be sure to read the Techniques section and the individual project instructions thoroughly before you begin. Use two strands of embroidery floss for all stitching unless otherwise stated.

1 Cut two 14" × 14" (36cm × 36cm) squares of the floral print.

2 Refer to the quilt instructions to make a butterfly block for the pillow front using one of the 14" × 14" (36cm × 36cm) square fabric pieces. You will use the other square for the pillow backing.

3 Refer to the General Instructions on page 18 to finish the pillow.

butterfly garden chenille wall hanging

fabric

COTTON PRINTS

Scraps of pink dot print (cheeks)

CHENILLE

Two 24" × 24" (61cm × 61cm) squares of pastel green chenille

14" × 14" (36cm × 36cm) square and four 5" × 5" (13cm × 13cm) squares of cream chenille

WOOL FELT

13" × 13" (33cm × 33cm) square of pink felt (butterfly wings)

Scraps of pink felt (small flowers and flower centers), cream felt (butterfly body), yellow felt (small flowers, dots on wings and flower centers) and pastel green felt (dots on wings)

supplies

23" × 23" (58cm × 58cm) square of quilt batting

DMC cotton embroidery floss: ecru, #3716 (pink), #368 (green) and #209 (lavender)

Regular or lightweight paper-backed fusible web

Seven ½" (13mm) lavender buttons and a ¼" (6mm) pink button

Two 1" (3cm) plastic loops (for hanging)

Materials and Tools (pages 8–10)

Pattern insert

Be sure to read the Techniques section and the individual project instructions thoroughly before you begin. Use two strands of embroidery floss for all stitching unless otherwise stated.

1 Cut two 24" × 24" (61cm × 61cm) squares of pastel green chenille. Cut a 14" × 14" (36cm × 36cm) square and four 5" × 5" (13cm × 13cm) squares of cream chenille.

2 Cut a 23" × 23" (58cm × 58cm) square of the quilt batting.
Note: Due to the unfinished edges, the batting should be approximately 1" (3cm) less in total size compared to the chenille squares.

3 Referring to the pattern insert, trace and cut the butterfly body from the cream felt, a wing piece, four small flowers and three small flower centers from the pink felt, four large dots, three small flowers and four small flower centers from the yellow felt and four small dots from the pastel green felt.

4 Follow the Fusible Web Appliqué instructions on page 13 to fuse two cheek circles onto the butterfly using the pink dot print.

5 Baste the 14" × 14" (36cm × 36cm) cream chenille square onto the center a pale green chenille square. There should be 5" (13cm) on each side of the square.

6 Blanket stitch around the cream chenille square with four strands of the pink floss.

7 Referring to the project photo and pattern for placement, baste the butterfly pieces onto the center of the cream chenille square.

8 Refer to the quilt instructions to embroider and add button nose.

9 Baste the three pink small flower centers onto the yellow flowers, then baste the flowers, overlapping the three edges of the cream chenille square. Blanket stitch around the flowers with the green floss and around the flower centers with the ecru floss. Stitch the lavender buttons onto the flower centers.

10 Baste the four 5" × 5" (13cm × 13cm) cream chenille squares, one onto each corner. Baste the four yellow small flower centers onto the pink flowers, then baste the flowers onto the centers of the four chenille squares. Blanket stitch around the flowers with the lavender floss and around the flower centers with the pink floss. Stitch the lavender buttons onto the flower centers.

11 Refer to the General Instructions on page 18 to complete the wall hanging. If desired, add a decorative running stitch around the four corners using four strands of the green floss.

Resources

The materials used in this book are basic sewing and craft supplies, which should be available at your local quilt, fabric and craft shops. However, in case you need extra help sourcing your supplies, I've included this handy list of online resources to assist you.

Beacon Adhesives, Inc.
Tel: 914-699-3405
www.beaconcreates.com
Fabri-Tac Permanent Adhesive

Chenille Magic
Tel: 952-831-3511
www.chenillemagic.com
If you are unable to find chenille at your local fabric or quilt shop, check out this great online resource.

DMC Corporation
Tel: 973-589-0606
www.dmc-usa.com
Cotton embroidery floss

Fairfield Processing
Tel: 800-980-8000
www.poly-fil.com
Quilt batting, pillow inserts and Poly-fil fiberfill stuffing

National Nonwovens
Tel: 413-527-3445
www.nationalnonwovens.com
Wool felt

Olfa
Tel: 800-962-6532
www.olfa.com
Rotary cutters, mats and rulers

Pellon Products
Tel: 877-817-0944
www.shoppellon.com
Wonder Under iron-on adhesive

Prym-Dritz Corporation
www.dritz.com
Disappearing-ink marking pens and Fray Check

Sullivans USA, Inc.
Tel: 800-862-8586
www.sullivans.net/usa/
Quilt basting spray and Fray Stop spray

Note: I actually use the 505 brand of fabric spray adhesive that is sold in Wal-Mart stores. However, I did not list the contact information for the actual company that manufacturers it because they are located in France: www.odif.com

Therm O Web
Tel: 800-323-0799
www.thermoweb.com
HeatnBond Lite iron-on adhesive

Wrights
Tel: 877-597-4448
www.wrights.com
Oodles of sewing products including rickrack and bias tape

Index

Check out these other inspiring titles from Krause Publications!

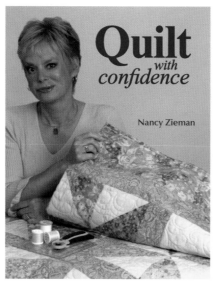

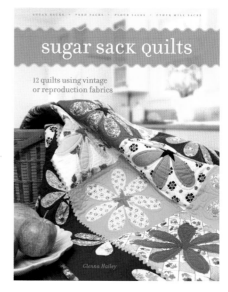

by Pam Lintott and Nicky Lintott

Create fifteen stunning quilts from fun and adorable jelly rolls of fabric. Whether you're an experienced quilter or someone new to the craft, you'll love these pretty projects.

ISBN-13: 978-0-7153-2863-7
ISBN-10: 0-7153-2863-8
Z2175
paperback, 128 pages

by Nancy Zieman

Learn quilting from sewing expert Nancy Zieman. Inside you'll learn how to select tools, organize your quilting area, use rotary techniques, seam and much more. It's all the confidence you need to start quilting and keep quilting.

ISBN-13: 978-0-89689-593-5
ISBN-10: 0-89689-593-9
Z1549
paperback, 144 pages

by Glenna Hailey

Create twelve pretty projects from reproduction fabrics or original feed sacks produced from 1930–1960. Learn the history of feed sacks as well as how to sew your own bed quilts and wall hangings using one-quarter and one-eighth yard cuts of fabric.

ISBN-13: 978-0-89689-521-8
ISBN-10: 0-89689-521-1
Z0850
paperback, 112 pages

These and other fine Krause Publications books are available from your local craft retailer, bookstore or online supplier. Or visit our Web site at www.mycraftivity.com.